MW00975134

BATTLE-TESTED FAITH

Battle-Tested Faith

Susan Sansalone

Sansalone Publishing, LLC

The author has tried to recreate events, locations, and conversations from her memories of them. In some instances, in order to maintain their anonymity, the author has changed the names of individuals and places. She may also have changed some identifying characteristics and details such as physical attributes, occupations, and places of residence.

Copyright © 2018 by Susan Sansalone

All rights reserved. No part of this book may be reproduced or transmitted in any form or by any means, electronic or mechanical, including photocopying, recording, or any information storage and retrieval system, without permission in writing from the publisher.

ISBN: 978-0-9998689-0-4

Library of Congress Control Number: 2018902970

10 9 8 7 6 5 4 3 2   0 3 2 0 1 8

Printed in the United States of America

☉This paper meets the requirements of ANSI/NISO Z39.48-1992 (Permanence of Paper)

Scripture quotations marked "NIV" are taken from the Holy Bible, New International Version®, NIV®.
Copyright © 1973, 1978, 1984 by Biblica, Inc.™ Used by permission of Zondervan. All rights reserved worldwide.

For there is nothing hidden that will not be disclosed, and nothing concealed that will not be known or brought out into the open.

—Luke 8:17 (NIV)

PREFACE

This is a story of how love can be a powerful force, and without love, whether it is withheld by a father, or husband, or vice versa, there comes rejection. That rejection takes a young girl into the arms of a loving God who changes her life and fixes her broken heart, driving her into the realization that while people will fail you, even your family, God won't. She goes from fear to faith and is determined to conquer her circumstances with the new boldness that develops from her faith. She operates with love and compassion, the two qualities withheld from her life by a father and a husband.

CHAPTER ONE

So what would you first remember if you thought back to your childhood? At what age do you think you recall incidents that would be identifying to you, good or bad? I can recall an incident when I was about four years old. My dad was a prominent real estate broker in Westchester, New York. He was adventurous and moved frequently because of his constant exposure to homes. We had a charming home in Bronxville, New York, and my father placed the house on the market. He was a man who made his own decisions, and my mother's advice or opinion was not something to be considered.

Before showing the house to an interested couple, he gave me specific orders to not mention that we were selling the house because of a recent water problem in the basement. The couple arrived at our house and toured our home, seemingly interested. They turned around and asked me a question pertaining to moving, and with that question I proceeded to give them an answer. Again, keep in mind that I was only four years old. I looked up with much innocence and said, "My daddy said we are selling this house because we have a terrible water problem."

The reaction, as you can well imagine, was not good. I cannot recall every detail, obviously, but enough to remember my father did not handle it well. The couple left the house.

Within minutes of their departure, my father's hand struck my frail little body and I flew across the room into my favorite green chair. The chair and I fell backward, and my mouth was bleeding profusely. His violent temper was uncontrollable. I survived, of course, not recalling the outcome of their decision, but the memory of our little Bronxville home was not a good one. So much for first recollections. The sad part of looking back is not the mistakes my father made, but growing up with the realization that he never believed he had made a mistake.

Then again, on a happier note, there are positive memories I can recall. I will always be thankful to my father for giving me a great appreciation for music. He put a microphone in my hand when I was five years old and recorded me singing on his radio station. He was detailed as to how he wanted a song sung. Diction was important to him, and he would make certain my t's were pronounced accurately and that I would hold my notes without cutting them off. We would spend hours at a time recording music on his reel-to-reel tape recorder, which at that time was the best of equipment. Looking back, I can appreciate being raised in a home with music, because now music plays a huge part in my life. I write, compose, and perform my own songs, and I have made my own CD.

My mother was very gifted. She had a beautiful voice and could hit high notes at such a smooth level. She was so special in many ways. She didn't have any say-so about anything, which as I look back was damaging in a way all of its own. She wanted desperately to keep peace in every situation, but in reality that was a delusional approach, especially when my father ruled the roost to a degree of insanity.

I had a timidity about me, or perhaps the right word would be fear. I would not say there was anything unusual about this fear, especially when every day my father would tell me the worst things that would happen to me if I were to do this or that. Unfortunately, this continual lifestyle had its toll, which was to manifest in severe physical problems later on. My father would make a point, for example, that if I was innocently going to the store with a friend for bubble gum, there was a good chance some man would kidnap us, rape us, and discard our bodies somewhere. To some, this would seem like an exaggeration, but it is not. It is every bit of the truth. There was a vile description of destruction to every move I would make. If I took a walk, for sure someone would be following me. If I drove alone at night, someone would follow me home and stalk me. If I stayed home alone, someone would break in and attack me. This was a continual way of life for me. My father constantly instilled fear, fear, and more fear. Perhaps, as I look back, he did this to manipulate me and bring himself more control and power. Maybe he figured the more he could scare me, the more I would never leave and be with anyone but him. I am convinced of that now.

I was quite talented growing up, and I had several gifts. I was athletic and seemed to always have a natural ability for certain sports. Since I was very young, my father would always have a new set of the best golf clubs under the Christmas tree, along with golf balls and a new golf bag. He would also have bowling balls, a bowling bag, shoes, and everything I would need to become a top-notch bowler. He himself was good at whatever he would teach me, using himself as an example. He was a great golfer, a great bowler, and he also sung with much passion, romance, and dedication. He spared no expense at developing my talent, especially with bowling.

I got involved and participated in several major tournaments in the Westchester County area, and then branched out to the metropolitan areas. I toured frequently to other states as I worked to the professional calling my father had laid out for me. I was good at bowling, scoring in an unusual way for a frail, young child. I started competing at the age of eight and won every "Westchester Metropolitan Bowling Champion" title for several years. I will always remember our home wallpapered in my newspaper articles. I was the little brunette beauty who could beat every man at any size and any age. I must admit, I wish that pattern in my life had continued.

I was a threat to anyone who competed against me, though I can't honestly say I enjoyed the fame. My father was breathing down my neck every day to perform without making any mistakes. He was a typical sports father, and it was important for him to receive glory in all my winnings. He was on a mission to make me a professional, even buying our own bowling alley and making me bowl twenty-five to thirty games a day. He put a lot of pressure on me. There was no fun to be remembered through all this, because in the course of my bowling career, he sent me to a private Catholic school, quite a distance from our house, which he personally drove me to every day. He was anything but religious or God-conscious, but it was another way of somehow not letting me be a part of the real world. The nuns were strict, and growing up between them all day and my father at night was not a good experience.

My mother, on the other hand, I adored. If I never knew anyone else in my life (and I rarely did), there was nothing as pleasant as being with my mother. She was my best friend and the sweetest, kindest woman God ever made. She was where I would feel safe (to a point). She had the most beautiful spirit and never thought of herself. She loved her family with all her heart and soul and put herself last. She was fearful of my father, which made life more difficult because she couldn't be assertive in areas where she needed to be. I needed her to protect me in several situations, which was impossible for her to do, but I loved her no matter what.

My bowling career continued into my teenage years, and I still traveled with Mom, Dad, and Grandma. My mother was also a good bowler and golfer. I had reached the point of being interested in boys, like any normal teenager, and they were interested in me too. It was one of the most challenging stages in my life, because I went to an all-girls high school in addition to my father not permitting me to date. He was extremely unreasonable, and there was no doubt that I was cheated of any normal teenage life. I wanted so desperately to be included, but I was forbidden to have any girlfriends, and even if I had an acquaintance, my father was such an overseer that nobody wanted to be friends with me. I had access to boys at the bowling alley, but that was all business and no fun, especially since my father owned the business.

Please don't misunderstand, I really did love my father. I would have done anything to please him, but that was just not possible. I was and still am an affectionate person, but hugs, kisses, and "I love yous" were foreign to me. My mother and father did not express any affection toward one another while I was growing up, and they did not express it to me. I needed my father's love and desired it with all my heart. He would never talk to me but at me, and I remember going to bed every night and wishing he would come in the room and kiss me goodnight.

I was now approaching sixteen years old, the age I could be signed up as a legitimate professional bowler. My name, no doubt, was out there, and even the *New York Post* had written about me several times. AMF *and* Brunswick were going to sign me up, and my big-time career would begin. It was not the desire of my heart, as all I wanted was to go to a high school dance and a football game at the local public high school. I remember how close I came to signing the papers. At that point, I had been televised several times as a junior bowler, and they would use me as a mascot for the big tournaments. Some of my own trophies were larger than I was. I had accomplished everything my father wanted of me until that point, until sickness struck me over and over again.

It's hard to know where to begin, but I recall clearly the severe stomachaches I would get as a child. Looking back now, as an adult, so much of it was related to my fear growing up and the stomach pains I would get as soon as my father walked through the door. There was a tension I would not wish on anybody, but it was something I had no control over.

One incident I failed to mention was the story of my first love. I think we all can relate to what a special love that is, and it is as real as ever, especially when you are sixteen. I was crazy about a boy, and he was just as crazy about me. I met him when I was fifteen and he was seventeen. He was dating my cousin, and he took one look at me—trust me, it was a connection like one of my favorite movies, *Splendor in the Grass*. We started to see each other as much as humanly possible, with the way my father was. My father knew him well and was aware how crazy we were about each other. We would occasionally go to high school dances together and have a great time. He was the captain of the football team at the local public high school. It was a big deal for me to even go to a game, since I came from an all-girls school. He loved bowling and was so proud of me. He was handsome and patient, even though, thanks to my father, he had a lot to deal with every time he wanted to date me. The high school football games were so much fun, but I had a curfew in the middle of the afternoon. I would have given anything to be a cheerleader and take a school bus like normal kids did.

My father's paranoia was becoming unbearable, and my limitations on seeing my boyfriend were ridiculous. If we went to a dance, my father would come and watch us the entire evening. I remember my father peering through the fence one night at an outside dance function. Even when we didn't know he was there, he would follow us around to the local library on Saturday afternoons. My boyfriend's patience was remarkable, especially when he could have any beautiful cheerleader and never have to deal with this. He really did care for me. Everyone in town was aware of my life. My father was this big real estate broker who also owned the local bowling alley, and any guy who wanted to date me couldn't, because I had the reputation of having a crazy father. I was quiet back then, and my father had no reason to treat me this way, except in his own sick imagination.

Well, now for the good part—or, should I say, the worst part. One night there was going to be a sweet-sixteen party at a girl's house. My father knew the family well and knew they would be present throughout the entire party, upstairs and downstairs. He had also restricted me to only seeing my boyfriend once a month. My mother, quite honestly, was well aware of how out of control my father was being, and when necessary would personally escort me to a date without his knowledge. The party was going to be on a Saturday night, and my father said I could go on the condition that I did not remain with my boyfriend during the course of the evening. How ridiculous can you get? I told my father I would be with Billy if that would make him happy. Fine.

I proceeded to attend this wholesome party with the parents' supervision, great food, fifties music, lights, and everything perfectly situated for any parent, even mine. I was having a great time, not realizing the hell that was to confront me. I was sitting on the couch with a few friends, including my boyfriend. Everything was fine. My father entered these lovely people's home in the middle of the party to spy on me. He walked down the steps to the basement only to find his daughter sitting there conducting herself in a fine manner as usual with friends on the couch. He grabbed me and slapped me, knocking me down in front of several teenagers who started to scream and cry at this outrage. The host's parents came down, her father trying to hold my father back from killing me. My boyfriend was devastated, especially since he could not help me with this abusive situation. Nobody knew what hit that place. My father had embarrassed me for no reason whatsoever. He was screaming uncontrollably, calling me a liar, and he started to pull me out of the house. I was crying so much and was so scared to leave. I knew he would take me home and beat me. The father of the girl hosting the party would not allow my father to take me home, thank God. The embarrassment was unbelievable. The scenes looked like something from a terrible movie as my father escorted me from the house. The girl's father would not let my father get in the car with me alone and drove home with us. He arranged for someone to pick him up when he arrived at our home. My father had destroyed this girl's sweet-sixteen party, along with his own reputation, as usual, as an abusive father. The party was ruined, never to be forgotten. Believe it or not, until this day, anyone who attended that party will still bring it up as a horrible night in that town.

I was taken into the house like some sort of criminal. I desperately did not want this girl's father to leave me alone. I wanted to be anybody's daughter in this world except my father's. This man was a wonderful father to his children and was upset that he had to leave me alone. He had no authority, as he was not my father, but he was so compassionate. It broke his heart to leave me. He was stern with my father over the issue, but nothing could be done.

My poor, precious mother did not know what hit her when we arrived. My father was violent and uncontrollable, and the punishment was unimaginable. I was not allowed out except for school, which was already like a convent, for one year under any conditions. My father took all my clothes away, leaving me with just my school uniform. I did not get out much as it was, but you cannot imagine the seclusion. I was allowed to bowl, but getting back to what I mentioned before, I was becoming ill from time to time. It became impossible for me to sign any contracts with AMF or make any serious commitment to my bowling career. Truthfully, I could have cared less. I wanted so much to just have some sort of normal life, but that was never to happen, not ever.

I failed to mention prior to this that my father was a big gambler. We had to deal with the daily consequences of whether he won or lost at anything, from cards to bowling to track. Our life depended on his winnings and his moods.

I would go to school every day with a knot in my stomach and nothing to look forward to. My boyfriend and I would exchange frequent letters at school, through a mutual friend, but we missed each other very much. I wanted to see him, but it was impossible. Time had passed, and I can't say I remember each detail exactly, but eventually my boyfriend had to go into the service. He finished high school and went off to Vietnam. I recall my father sitting down with him at the bowling alley and apologizing for the scene, but the damage had already been done. We did see each other occasionally, but things changed and off he went into the service.

My bowling career had terminated due to illness, and soon after all this I too graduated from high school. I was so anxious to get out of school. My junior and senior years were horrible. I missed dances, picture-taking, and every event possible due to illness. I had terrible stomach problems. My first surgery was at sixteen for an ovarian cyst. Then shortly after that I had an emergency appendectomy. These surgeries were still not solving my constant abdominal pain. I was a very unhappy young person, and the restrictions on my social life were beginning to take a toll.

Chapter Two

I had finally completed high school with much expectation, but I can't say I had any great plans for my future. College was not something to be considered. I did not like school, and I did not have any desire to continue my education. I went to work immediately following high school.

I was good at business skills, so that is what I pursued. I did not explore many areas at that time of my life. I can't say I had any particular desire to do anything. I knew I was talented in certain areas, but I had nothing to make a career out of.

I didn't have many friends and I wasn't interested in the bar scene. I kept to myself most of the time. I still loved being around people, but I didn't have much in common with most of them. I never enjoyed drinking, but I loved to dance. Unfortunately, it was difficult to find that enjoyment apart from the bar and clubs.

My father required twenty dollars a week from me out of my salary. I had no problem with that. I had the advantage of living a comfortable life as far as material things were concerned. My father was successful with money; however, with his gambling habits, holding on to it was another story.

I was now eighteen years old, and I continued to battle physical problems on and off while going to work. I was still living a stressful life, not being able to come and go as I pleased.

One evening I met someone at a Friday-night church dance. We started to date on a steady basis, and I fell hard for him. He seemed to feel the same way about me, and we were definitely serious about each other. I brought him home to meet my father, who had been critical of everybody and skeptical that anyone would be good enough. My boyfriend worked for his father in the construction business. I tried reasoning with my father—all I wanted to do was date him, not marry him, and I wanted the freedom to make my own mistake, if that was what I was doing.

I was eighteen years old and a working young woman. I did not run around with guys. I was particular and sensible, and I had strong Christian beliefs, even as a young girl. I cared for my boyfriend so much and wanted to be with him. However, my father was an irrational man and had no moral standards whatsoever. He was unfaithful to my mom most of his married life, and I did not respect his opinion on matters in which I conducted myself better.

Heeding his advice—or should I say, orders—was not the right way to handle the situation. I was kindly asking for my father to back off and let me be free to make my own decisions. He threatened me in his usual insane manner. He told me if I didn't stop dating this boy, he would drive me to work, take the car away from me, and make my life miserable. We know he was good at doing this, and control and manipulation were his only tactics. I was still experiencing all the stomach pains, and the more he exercised his control, the worse they became. My mother stayed out of it, and there was no reasoning with the situation at all.

I was eighteen, and this man treated me like I was ten.

I remember retreating to my bedroom after his new rules were about to be enforced. I started to recall the year he had kept me from my first boyfriend. I got sick to my stomach and could not bear to continue living like this. I wanted out of this life and away from this man, and I did not know what to do. I had saved up $1,500 in the bank, which was a lot at that time, from the short time I had been working, but I had no place to turn. I spoke to my boyfriend's father on the phone that night and turned to him. He was well aware of my father. He offered limited advice, but he could not help me.

I went to bed with my usual intention of going to work the next day. I was no longer allowed to even drive myself to work, so my mother would drive me every day. This was my father's instruction for as long as I was dating this boy. How sick and demented could a father be? I arrived at work in the morning, and by the end of my work day at 4:30 p.m., my mother was to pick me up. I had reached a breaking point in my life. I couldn't possibly imagine returning home to spend one more night in my father's house, so I did something completely out of character for me. To this day I can't believe it happened, but thinking back to the pain I was living in, I can.

I worked all day and made arrangements for my boyfriend to pick me up instead of my mother. We had no idea where we would go. I was absolutely petrified. I knew by five o'clock my mother would wonder where I was. I was so upset because I would never, ever hurt my mother, but I just could not go home anymore. My boyfriend and I drove and drove and drove. There was no plan and no destination. All I knew was that I could not go back home.

We drove through New Jersey, and before you knew it, Pennsylvania, and we kept going. It was dark by now, and I knew no matter what I could never turn back. I was paralyzed with fear, but either way it was a no-win situation. Again, keep in mind I was not an independent person at all. I also want to mention that I had withdrawn my $1,500 from the bank—the boy I was running away with certainly had no money. We were well into the late evening by this point, but we kept driving and driving. I remember the song "Nowhere to Run" playing. That was me. I had closed out my bank account and was running away from home at eighteen years old, and I had brought nothing except my toothbrush.

I had never gone anywhere without my parents. I had no experience being independent, but I was determined to never return to my father's control. I was a desperate young girl and there was no way out for me, ever, except to run away. I had tried to reason with my father the night before, and I remembered clearly asking him to just let me grow up and date. I needed to find out for myself about life, and if I dated the wrong person, then I would have to learn from my own lessons. I tried to explain that his method of locking me up was insane, and if he didn't let me be a normal working eighteen-year-old, I would not come home the next day. He threatened me and laughed at me, like he knew only too well that his little frightened daughter would and never could run away. I ran to my bedroom crying hysterically to call my boyfriend, even speaking to his father about the situation. We had no major plans other than getting in the car after work and driving away.

Midnight was approaching, and we were somewhere in the state of Virginia. I was so exhausted and somewhat in shock. What had I done? I could never turn around and go home again, and I didn't want to. But I didn't want to be running away state to state with this boy; I just wanted to date him. We were crazy about each other, but young and naïve, and I, for one, had not dated a lot and was not very experienced about the facts of life. Oh yes, I knew some things, but not what I should have known by the age of eighteen. I was way too sheltered. Though I was somewhat grateful for that at times, it wouldn't make a good ending.

I knew one thing for certain, and it was that I had loved God with my whole heart and soul ever since I was a little girl. I was a devout Catholic girl and never missed Mass with my mother growing up, nor a holy day of obligation. I had something deeper than any religion I was ever taught, and that was a genuine love and fear of God. He was so real to me, and I believed in His protection and prayed to Him on a daily basis. Oh yes, there was all the religion and all the rules I obeyed, but still there was something deeper in my heart for God than all the traditions I had been taught.

CHAPTER THREE

Midnight arrived, and it was obvious that we had to stop someplace and sleep. We pulled up to a place; I cannot recollect exactly where and what part of what state we were in. It didn't matter. I was far away from home, and I feared my father had every police department on the lookout to pick me up and throw me in some jail. Of course my fears were legitimate—everything he taught me in life was about fear, so what else could I possibly think?

We checked into a motel with twin beds. There was still an aspect of shock to this whole ordeal. What had I done? I knew why I had done it, but nothing diluted the fear of my present situation. For the sake of my story, I will give my boyfriend a name. Every story has to name its characters, so we will now call him Tony. That isn't, of course, his real name, but it can certainly depict a dark-haired Italian boy with drop-dead looks and a real Italian heritage like myself. He was tough and young, and honestly, he did have a lovely family. His father was a nice man and was also handsome. His sister was kind and gentle, and his mother was a strong Italian woman who wore the pants in his family. Unlike my mother and father, his mother was the boss.

When we got to the motel, I was upset and frightened. I never forgot my religious foundation, and I refused to sleep anyplace but in my own twin bed. Tony knew where I was coming from, and I took my stand about never, ever sleeping with someone until I was married. Again, let me mention that I did not know all the facts of life. I choose not to get specific. I cried and cried and cried all night and hardly slept at all. We had no change of clothes, and fear gripped me tighter and tighter. Morning arrived, and our destination at this point was Florida. We both knew we could never turn back. My money was all we had, and we had to stretch it as much as possible. I kept thinking of my poor mother and how she had tried to help avoid this horror I was enduring, but she too did not deserve the suffering my father inflicted. I wanted my mother so much. I loved her and wished she was with me more than anybody in the world. I wished I could have had a life with my mother somewhere, anywhere without my father.

I didn't go one day in life without strife, and we all suffered needlessly because of him. I mentioned briefly before that my father was unfaithful to my mother. That was putting it mildly. He had a mistress who was always with us, as though she were his second wife. She went everywhere with us, and she had even known me since I was born. She also had her own family and children, but still she led a double life with our family. It was strange and stressful, and my mother, of course, knew. There was nothing women could or would do back then about things.

It was interesting to observe and experience the control my father had over all our lives, and the lack of control he had over his own where it concerned morals and conduct. He lived the way he wanted. He was with whomever he chose and purchased whatever he wished without consulting with my mother on anything. I remember so vividly when my father picked a private school for me to attend when I was young. I was approaching the third grade, if I recall correctly, and he chose this Catholic school, which was quite a distance from where we lived. He would drive me to school and back—forty-five minutes each way—and he would never speak to me. I never had a conversation with him going or coming. Instead, he would always listen to the news on the radio and ignore me. He would drop me off at this private school, which was not large and was actually just a house, not a real school. It was run by nuns, and there were only about ten kids per classroom. The nuns were so strict. When we had lunch, we were not allowed to speak to each other until one of the nuns rang a little bell. When the bell rang, we could speak, and when the bell rang again, we had to stop speaking.

I hated being so far away from home, and I wanted to take a school bus and go up the street to school like other kids, but that was never going to happen. I desperately wanted a normal life, but he never asked me what I wanted, nor did he care. When school was out at the end of the day, I had to wait for him, his mistress, or my mother to pick me up, and then the long drive home. I would always hope my mother would pick me up, because I knew we would talk and I would be happy. I loved her so.

When I would get home, I never had girlfriends I played with or activities I enjoyed. I did not like attending this school, but this is where I would be throughout elementary school. My activities would be dictated by my father, either bowling or golfing, whichever he designated at the time.

As hard as it might seem to believe, I did love my father very much. The cry of my heart was that I wanted my father to love me. He thought in his ways he was showing me his love—through his control, perhaps. He was not a person who would demonstrate any sort of affection to my mother or myself. I certainly recall several occasions where my father, who as I mentioned earlier was a gambler, would return home from a late night of cards or bowling, and we would be victims of his winning or his losing. When he won, though, he won big. I would come into the kitchen the next morning, and there would be a pile of money placed on the table. He was generous with his winnings and never withheld anything that material things could buy. But if he lost, there would be no money, and the worst of it would be his mood. He would be miserable, and of course, that would affect us.

My father would set up match games for me to bowl head to head, meaning one on one, for maybe one hundred dollars a game. He enjoyed setting me up to compete, and I did pretty well when the pressure was on. I was competitive when it came to sports. I liked to win, I wanted to win, and I played to win. I did win most of the time, and my father enjoyed the glory all the way, but when I lost, it was not fun. He made my life miserable.

CHAPTER FOUR

Morning had arrived, and Tony and I had checked out of the motel. I was exhausted and had had very little sleep. We proceeded to drive farther south toward Florida, and I had still had no contact with my parents. Naturally, I wouldn't have unless I called home, and I knew that was not possible, or at least not probable. The only option left was for us to be married in one of these hick towns along the way. Turning back was not going to happen, and unless I was married, I could no longer return home with my parents. We didn't plan any of this, but took it moment by moment. Finally, we hit a destination in North Carolina. I never knew anyplace but New York, so you can just imagine how uncomfortable all this was. We went to a justice of the peace, and to get right to the point, we were married.

Frightened was putting it mildly. This was all like a bad dream I wouldn't wake up from anytime soon. It was late afternoon, the weather was very hot, we were out in the middle of nowhere, and we were going into this house to get married. We followed all the protocol, and it was simple enough. So be it. It was done.

We continued our drive toward Florida as night arrived. We stopped again at a motel, only this time, reality was to set in. It is difficult for me to put in writing what my evening was like, because the actual experience was so horrifying I can't capture the details. I will do my best. While I choose not to get specific, I will say very candidly that I did not know the facts of life regarding marriage, nor did I know what to expect when I arrived at this motel.

Tony, on the other hand, was a frustrated young man who was definitely not on the same page as a frightened young girl running away from home. He had a good relationship with his parents and was not experiencing the same terror as I was.

This was some rural town we had stopped in, and the motel was pathetic, to say the least. We checked into the room, showered, and cleaned up after a shocking day. I remember coming out of the bathroom trying to be the best little bride under these circumstances, even though my body was shaking like a leaf. I will never forget Tony's first words to me: "Get on the bed." It was so demanding I thought I had misunderstood. He said it again and again. I froze like a statue, petrified, and in a split second he threw me onto the bed. He had turned into a savage and exploded in anger within minutes as he proceeded to get on top of me. I didn't know what to do. It was bad enough that I hadn't known what to do before, but obviously neither did he. He forced himself on me, full of his sexual frustrations, and was blinded with such rage that he started to hit me. I was screaming at the top of my lungs and within seconds, someone was knocking at the door. I ran into the bathroom holding my breath from hysteria while he answered the door and made up some excuse for the commotion. They threatened to call the police if it happened again, which was a blessing in disguise, because now he had to stop hitting me. I had been thrown from one end of the motel room to the other, and my body was so bruised. I felt like I was in hell and there was nothing I could do about it.

I had not witnessed this anger in Tony before, and obviously the extent of our sex life had been quite limited beforehand. A drive-in movie and kissing, but we had never attempted sexual relationships of any sort. The sad part is how strict my father was with me, and again, for no reason, because I was never conducting myself in a manner that warranted his restrictions. I had seen Tony get mad, but it would be over losing a game of pool. Still, I had felt safe enough to be with him.

That night was a complete horror. Nothing transpired sexually, but the fighting was unbearable and his behavior was frightening. I was in the middle of some hick town in the South with Tony, and I was legally now his wife at eighteen years old.

The next day was a new day, but a sad one. I had no father to call and nowhere to run or hide. We continued our journey to Florida because there was no alternative. I was the saddest person on the planet. I was frightened enough, but now, I was driving and felt like a young girl who had been raped. I kept thinking that this wouldn't have happened if I weren't so religious. I had been in a motel with him the night before and if I sinned I would have known this and never gotten married? How ignorant, but I felt so spiritually and physically raped that I couldn't help but wonder if I was the type to sleep around and had experience would I have had to face the consequences of virginity the way I did?

Of course this wasn't about virginity. But how could I not think that? Tony was an immature young man desperate for sex, and he needed to sleep around. He took all his ignorance and imaginations out on me. He hung around other guys. He didn't know what to do or how to act. He was a maniac, not the handsome young boy I had been dating who adored and protected me. What had happened? He had turned into Satan in a second—and I was married to him. It was evident that I wouldn't leave my father to run away and be with someone who would hit me. He had never done anything like this before. He hasn't been dating me all those months for sex. Why hadn't he just gone out with a girl and gotten what he wanted? He wanted me and swore he loved me. Sex was not a priority in our relationship because we had other things in common, so this was a complete shock to me. Nobody would run away like this just for sex! I tried over and over again to reason this out, but it was horrible. It would only get worse as time went on.

CHAPTER FIVE

It is difficult to put in words what transpired. Tony was a young boy, not even a man, and had no clue as to how to conduct himself in a situation like this. I admit my own lack of experience in this area, and quite frankly, I'm not a bit ashamed of it. This was who I was. If he wanted a quick fix from a girl, he certainly took the long way around. I was not in bed for sex. I was an eighteen-year-old girl who wanted to spend the rest of her life with a husband and have a peaceful family life. I was not ignorant to a wife's duties; if anything, I was quite conscious of being pretty and sexy and special. I would sound corny and pathetic to most people, but I believed in staying a virgin until marriage. I was not perfect, by any means. I was just as human as the next person. I had to resist temptation too, even though such occasions rarely arose. I was not any angel walking around with a halo on my head, but God as my judge, I was a virgin. That is so hard for me to say for some reason. In today's society it would be scorned and made fun of, but it is God's law.

I was prepared in every other aspect to be a good wife, and it was unfortunate that if Tony had the qualities of a good person, we could have had a future together. I was not interested by any means in dating others. As I mentioned previously, I could not care less about being with different boys. I was a one-man woman, and the right man would have my loyalty and devotion forever.

The evening turned out to be a disaster. It was nothing but a replay of the night before. There was no affection, or kissing, or any emotional contact. He proceeded to get on top of me and perform a sexual act. I was more interested in being loved and caressed and held, all the love that would make for a beautiful evening. He was anxious and forceful and just wanted sex. He was harsh and cruel in every way, and I will never forget the painful experience of this person, who was now a stranger, on top of me. I struggled, yet he persisted. It was the worst experience of my life. It was mentally, emotionally, and physically abusive.

I can still remember the motel room looking out over the ocean. I loved Miami Beach. My father took us every year growing up at Easter vacation. It was a three-day drive from New York at that time. I had looked forward to it every year. Now I was sitting in a motel feeling shattered, alone, and desperate. I had never meant to run away. I just wanted to date. I couldn't help but think how I had been forced to run away, that or be my father's prisoner. What were my options? I had run away with one person, and now he was somebody else.

My honeymoon night was horrible. Most teenagers have a better experience in the back seat of a car. I was numb. I felt raped more now than the night before because Tony had forced himself on me much more. It was a painful, agonizing experience that I couldn't shake from my entire being.

CHAPTER SIX

We are now in the fourth day of being gone. I was miserable and wish I had a father I could run to and cry on his shoulder. I decided to call home. I wanted my mother so badly. I attempted to call several times at a phone booth, but I hung up every time from fear. I couldn't bear my father screaming at me and informing me that he had disowned me. Fortunately, his sick threats didn't matter to me anymore. I felt like my life was over. The damage was done. I was legally married to this young boy and I was ruined for life. Every dream of a beautiful wedding day and all that came with it was over. It was never to happen, and even if I hadn't run away, it still would never have happened for me because of my father.

I mustered up the courage to call home late that afternoon. I wanted my mother to answer the phone, but that was nothing new. I always wanted my mother to answer the phone. I finally made the call with a heavy heart. I had to pretend I was okay, and I would continue to live that lie to my parents from that day on. The last thing I could do was tell the truth.

My father answered the phone. I held back my tears and courageously spoke to him. "Hi, Dad."

I trembled from head to toe. I thought he would scream or hang up or something cruel, because that was his nature. To my surprise, he did not react that way. I was shocked and grateful. I had been gone four days, and they had never heard a word from me. I did not say much, and my voice was quivering. He asked me where I was and said he had been communicating with Tony's parents as to our whereabouts. Tony had not called home yet at this point.

For the first time in my life, my father was not yelling at me. He was upset, but he said there was nothing any of us could do now except deal with the situation. It was a brief phone call, and we hung up. I stood in the phone booth all alone and cried and cried and cried. Why couldn't he speak calmly to me before, instead of threatening my life all the time?

Needless to say, as it turns out, my father had already begun his mission to control me and Tony by now. It was only a few days before all hell broke loose, and my father planned our every move from there on out. I had honestly thought, for a split second, that maybe he was sincerely going to support me for once and walk through this with me. Instead, he accelerated his control. He knew he held every card because we had no money to support ourselves. The fire would now grow hotter and hotter, only I was in this fire with Tony and my father.

I should have known when I spoke to him that if he wasn't reacting violently, he was up to something. Sure enough, that was the case. Control was what he knew best, and he was plotting to set this thing up according to his way. Only this time he had met his match with Tony's mother. There would be nothing but war from here on in. I told you earlier that Tony's mother wore the pants in his family, and believe me, she was not going to take any of my father's nonsense. This was not the kind of woman my father was used to, and believe me, my father was used to women. They obviously had begun their disagreements and plans for both of us. I wasn't looking forward to returning to New York, nor did I want to spend another day with Tony in Florida or any other place. This was a mess beyond words.

We remained in Florida for the duration of the week and a couple days into the second week. When we started our journey back to New York, nothing had changed between me and Tony. I was to return home to find out what awaited me and now live a lie that I was happy and doing just fine. I wished I could have told my father the truth right then, but once again, his actions forced me to continue the path I was on.

CHAPTER SEVEN

The drive was a long one back, and we made very few stops this time. I had butterflies in my stomach and didn't have a clue what I was returning to. I mentioned early on that I had a lot of sickness after the age of fifteen. I had had two abdominal operations at this point of my life, but I still fought stomach pains frequently. I had an ovarian cyst removed at sixteen and still had gynecological problems on and off in addition to intestinal problems. I can assure you the stress was certainly adding to the legitimate issues I was confronting.

We arrived home and all of us congregated in my parents' home. I was, as usual, being treated like a child, though Tony's parents treated him just fine. My father and his mother had come up with a way to support us. Tony would continue to work in construction with his father, and they signed a lease for a small apartment down the street. Quite frankly, I think Betty (Tony's mother) and my father were enjoying the journey. They had all the say-so in everything. They picked out the furniture, television, and all the necessities. We just had to settle in and do what they said. They owned it all.

Betty was a tough, insensitive woman, while her husband was kind like my mother. She was bitter toward me, which was sad because I always liked them all. She made it clear, however, that she ran things along with my father. It was disgusting, and I was becoming quite ill at times without anybody knowing. I would double up with my stomach pains. I had gotten a good job, like I had before, and did well as a working woman. I made decent money and made a significant contribution to our situation. I was great at business skills and performed well at running an office. My phone skills were great too, and sales was something I would always excel at. I tried to settle in to the little eighteen-year-old married woman I was, and I kept a lovely, lovely apartment.

Tony was becoming more and more difficult to live with and could not settle in at all. Of course, everything had to be kept a secret because our parents were now supporting us in our endeavors. The last thing I could do was speak out on the truth of this marriage. He was a wild young boy who needed to sow his oats, and now he was going to do all of it behind our parents' backs. There was nothing I could do about it. He would get drunk, even though he never drank before, ever. I hated drinking and smoking. Those two things kept me out from behind bars, and nothing could make me want that lifestyle. My father, even with all his vices, would always brag that he didn't smoke or drink. It was true. He hated those things, and frankly, so did I.

Some nights Tony would not come home at all. When he did, he was mean and drunk. He became more abusive, and it was obvious that his life was becoming worse and worse. His friends were not a good group, and I didn't have friends at all. My father was against that too. Tony would still throw me on the floor and try to force sex on me to get the satisfaction he needed. I was getting sicker and sicker and thinner and thinner. He wanted out, and he said he would beat me until I would tell my father. He knew I would die before telling my father the truth, so that was his biggest weapon against me. He dislocated my jaw one evening, and I spent the night in the emergency room alone. I would never, ever call my family. I was so beaten one night that I couldn't get the bloodstains off the rug. I was petrified someone would see it when they came over. I cooked, ironed, cleaned, and worked, and I grew up real fast. I was still a great homemaker through it all, but it was difficult being alone with my stomach problems.

Our lives continued to go in this same direction for months, and in the interim preparations were made to be married in the Catholic Church. I was close to God, as I mentioned early on, and I was a devoted Catholic (at that time). We had been married by the justice of the peace, but now we would proceed with a small, regular wedding in a comfortable Italian church I was familiar with. Now we would be married by the priest. I went forward making some plans, but like I said, I only had a couple of friends, and we would keep it small even though Tony's family was much larger than mine. I wore a short, plain white dress with a plain hairpiece. My cousin would be my maid of honor. My father could have cared less about a church wedding, but for my mother and Tony's mother, it was important. Most of all, it was important to me.

The plans were made, and I had a great Italian priest unlike anybody I had ever met. Priests and nuns could be pretty rigid about things, but he was a wonderful human being and someone who would represent the Church in a special way. The ceremony took place, and then we proceeded to a restaurant for some celebration. I knew I wasn't going anywhere in this marriage, so getting the Church's blessing and making this official was all I knew to do. My faith and relationship with God were the most important things in my life, and finalizing this marriage with God's blessing was, to me, the right thing to do. The fact that everything was going wrong from the beginning did not change my plans to be married in the Church, because that's what I believed in. Did being married in the Church change my situation? Absolutely not. Things would continue as usual—if anything, they would get worse. I continued living my life alone with my problems and not involving anybody else. I had no choice.

I was an avid churchgoer, so going to Mass and communion were active parts of my life. I had often gone with my mother when I lived at home, but now I would go alone to this Italian church I had been married in. It was a warm church, and Father Francis was so down to earth. He was different from any priest I had ever known. I was more comfortable here than anyplace else.

My situation at home had grown worse. However, the difference was that I had opened up to this priest about the whole story, so now we had a mediator in the picture. I will always thank God for this man, because he was truly a God send. Just knowing I had opened up to someone I finally trusted was a huge relief for me. I went to speak with him often, and at one point he got Tony and I together to speak to us both. Talking to Tony was like beating a dead horse to death. He was a young, wise punk who was not on the same page as I was. He wasn't even the same person he had been a few months prior. He had turned into a complete monster.

There was no way he wanted help of any kind, not for himself, and much less for the two of us.

Father Francis was always there for me and stayed on top on this situation as best he could. I called him over to our apartment on occasions when Tony would get violent, and he would try to intervene without involving the police. After several months of trying to help and seeing what danger I was in, Father Francis had really had enough of Tony. He got tough and warned him that he would be in jail if this continued. He was not going to stand by and watch this anymore. Well, this was just what Tony wanted. The whole idea was to push me over the top so I would return to my father and this whole marriage would end.

Needless to say, after over eight months into this marriage, I was coming to the end of myself physically and mentally. I was very sick with abdominal pains, and they were getting worse. I had gone to a few doctors, but nobody could diagnose me properly. I had so many issues between my ovaries and intestines that I always bounced between the two problems. I had no intimate relationship with Tony, as he obviously had a sexual life outside our home. I was now in a position where I could no longer continue my life with him. Some might think this was great news, but the fact of the matter is, my life would now return to my father's tyrannical ways. Freedom would never be a reality.

Tony had thrown his last punch at me and knew this was the blow that would get me out. I could clearly remember him saying, "Go, just go, go ahead and tell your father. You have no choice. Go tell your father."

I went to the rectory at the church where Father was, and as usual, he was there for me. He also knew my time was up and comforted me with the fact that he would be there for me no matter what. The rectory was my sanctuary, and I wished I could have just moved in and hid under a statue or in the confessional box for the duration of my life. I couldn't have asked for a better friend and counselor than Father Francis. Little did I know, he would be one of my best friends for the rest of my life.

I now was confronted with my worst fear: going home to my father. How could this be possible? Well, the day arrived when I mournfully left my apartment and had to ask my parents if I could come back home. You don't get lower than this. My heart was pounding as I pulled up the driveway. It was probably pounding so loud because my heartbreak was so heavy—and now, it would only get worse. I was still fighting the stomach pains, and returning home was like a death sentence, even after almost a year with Tony.

I stood on the stoop and rang the bell. I had nothing with me, except my broken heart and failure stamped all over my face. As usual, I could have really used a hug. I had always wanted a hug. Who was I kidding? I did have a great imagination.

My father answered the door. He took one look at me and his sarcasm spewed out of his mouth. He was such a cruel human being that to this day, it is hard to believe. He looked at me and laughed and called my mother in the background. "Mary, guess who's here? Your daughter."

I walked inside with a heavy heart, and my father took over within seconds. He told me if I came back home, I would listen to him this time—or else! He never asked if I was okay, which I wasn't, of course. He didn't care what I had been through, nor did he choose to ask. He just took his position of control and manipulation and threats and laid them out on the table. It was the most heart-wrenching experience of my life.

It was cruel and evil, to say the least. Even writing about it doesn't do justice to the evil present in him at that moment. I went to my old bedroom upstairs and dropped on the bed, overcome with sadness. It was over, but it wasn't over at all. Oh God, it wasn't over at all. What would happen to me? I was sick, and I felt like I had been thrown into prison for something I didn't do.

CHAPTER EIGHT

I continued to work in Bronxville, New York, which I really did enjoy. Even so, I was losing weight and becoming more and more ill because of my stomach. I had seen doctors with my mother on several occasions, but nobody was helping me. Father Francis and I stayed in touch often, and our friendship grew and grew. Living with my father was every bit of the horror that I anticipated. He and Tony's mother were removing all the furniture from the apartment and grabbing their rightful belongings, as each one had distributed. It was disgusting, to say the least. You'd think it was their marriage that had broken up. Tony went back to live with his parents and lived like the bum he was. Now my father had his lawyer working to get this marriage annulled in the courts, and I had nothing to say about a thing. I would retire to my bedroom after work, in between being sick, and going to church remained my only relief.

The stress from the breakup was so bad between the parents that, looking back, I honestly don't know how I survived. His parents came over to the house one day with Tony and the scene was horrific. I came downstairs to the living room as they argued over their belongings. His mother started to bring up personal issues between me and

Tony, and she really went out of line. One detail vividly stands out to me: she started to put me down and embarrass me by saying to my father, "Your daughter couldn't even have sex with my son. You were so strict with her all these years, and she would have been better off if you had let her go out and learn the ropes on her own." Wow! That was painful. I remained paralyzed on the couch when she said that. My father turned to her and said, "There is no such thing as a frigid woman, just a stupid man."

Wow, again, he should know of all people. How humiliating that I was being discussed in my home, about such a personal issue, by these so-called adults. My father's remark was, obviously, to boast of himself and his manhood, and his response was clearly not on my behalf. Otherwise he would have silenced the whole conversation. Shame on them. It was horrible.

They pursued their arguments and I went to my room, devastated. Their greed continued for months and months as my body continued to break down. I was hospitalized on several occasions, and nobody could determine what was causing my pain. I was missing work more and more. I also had developed a great relationship with my boss, who was more concerned about my health than my job. He held my position when I was out sick, and was a really special friend to me through this. He knew the whole story and was a great man and influence in my life at that time. He was old enough to be my father, and I was good friends with his daughter, who also worked with me.

While all these negative circumstances were trying to swallow me up between hospital visits, Father Francis wanted me to pursue a church annulment. I had no idea what I was in for when I consented. I had never even thought about it. However, it seemed the right thing to do. He scheduled various appointments for me at St. Patrick's Cathedral in the city. The chancellery was there, along with the priests in charge of these matters. Again, please understand, I was only eighteen years old and I had been very ill. My father was dealing with the court annulment, and now I was in pursuit of a church annulment, all while losing weight and spending most of my time in the hospital.

I scheduled my first appointment with a priest. I had no idea what to expect or what kind of questioning would be on their agenda. I had one goal, and that was to get this annulment. I still have to admit I was naïve to what was going on, but when being questioned by this priest, I can tell you—it was shocking. The questions were so invasive and personal that I thought I had heard incorrectly.

I intend to be quite honest in revealing some of the questions I was confronted with. I was told that God would absolutely in no way forgive me and that I made my bed and would have to lie in it. I was accused of acting immorally. They would in no way accept my word that this marriage had not been consummated. I was questioned over and over again as to how much this man had penetrated my body, and I was to be exact and detailed in my response. They would not listen to the truth: that I had been terrified throughout the marriage and nothing had transpired sexually. I tried to prove my innocence, but they would not hear of it. After hours of interrogation, I was asked to leave as though I were the worst sinner on the planet.

I left hysterical and ran out of the church to Father Francis. He was devastated. He really was. He was upset at their conduct and scheduled me to have a meeting with another priest, whom he knew and believed would be more lenient.

I visited a second time, and again this priest was cruel and invasive in his questioning. I still look back and cannot believe I was sitting in this beautiful cathedral with priests floating around all over the place, only to learn they were sheep in wolves' clothing. I had no idea of this truth at the time. I was so young, and their approval meant everything. I walked out again, humiliated and broken, with a note saying I would have to be examined several times by the physicians of the church to prove my innocence.

I had been running around to my own doctors trying to find out why I was so sick, and now I was going to be examined by the church-designated physicians. I would have done anything for this annulment, so I naturally went forward. My first examination was grueling. I was inspected like a rape victim and judged like I was guilty of something criminal. It was horrible. There were to be several examinations, and believe me when I tell you there was not just one physician present.

I continued to follow every instruction the church gave me, until my abdominal pains became so bad that my parents had no choice but to rush me to a reputable doctor in the city. I can remember the pain so vividly, and I thought I was going to die. We walked into this office in the village, and the doctor was old and experienced, to say the least. He and his son, also a doctor, examined me. He couldn't touch my abdomen. He walked out of the room, picked up the phone, and called the biggest surgeon in the city and told him he would be sending a young girl over immediately. He asked this doctor to call him in an hour.

My parents rushed me to the other side of the city, where the line was out the door to see this surgeon. They took me in and this man examined me and called the other doctor. He had found a mass and told my parents I needed surgery right away. I was placed in a New York City hospital immediately. My parents were crying, even my father, and they were scared I was going to die.

I will get right to the point: I had the surgery. I was diagnosed with Crohn's disease. The operation was huge, and I will be honest with you, my life—at least the one I had up to this point—would only get worse. Many years I suffered with intestinal problems without a diagnosis, and nobody had helped me. I was in the hospital for a couple of weeks with tubes and my mother said you couldn't even walk into the room from the odor of the poisons coming out of the tubes. The doctor wanted to know if I had been out of the country. He was absolutely the finest, smartest, kindest, most brilliant doctor who would ever be found. I asked him why it was that nobody could ever find out what was wrong with me, and he could. He said experience. So now I had a good internist in the village and a brilliant surgeon on Park Avenue who would be my physicians. I was very fortunate. It wasn't common to have regional ileitis back then. President Eisenhower had this, and people were more aware of it because of him.

Father Francis came almost every day to visit me and give my parents a break to run out and get something to eat. I was so ill. The surgery was successful, though I felt anything but. This was a huge operation, so I wouldn't recover easily or quickly. I had a long road ahead of me. Apparently, stress was the worst factor. My life knew nothing else, of course. I could remember back to when Tony would not help me even though I would be doubled over. I would think I was going to die on the floor.

I continued to have problems with my ovaries through all this, and the situation got complicated when they added a gynecologist to the picture. The Crohn's surgery indicated my ovaries were somewhat diseased at nineteen years old, and four times the size of a normal ovary. The surgeon had expressed concern about my ovaries several times, and encouraged me not to wait long if I planned on ever having children.

I would go to the city two to three times a week for two years after the surgery. I had been placed on antibiotics and steroid therapy, but I was never well. I became so thin. I didn't look like the same girl. I was frail and weak, hardly ate, and when I did, I was sick. I had pernicious anemia after the surgery and septicemia (blood poisoning), and was hospitalized for treatment a few times after the surgery. I couldn't get my strength back. I would look in the mirror and hardly believe the skin and bones I had turned into.

I took a ride to my job in Bronxville one day to say hello to everybody while my boss held my job. I will never forget their faces when they saw me. I was told later they all thought I had leukemia.

I would hear my mother crying in her bedroom all the time. My mother never cried. I know she thought I was going to die.

I was visiting the surgeon twice a week now, and only God knows how blessed I was to have this doctor. He took care of me like I was his own child. He was concerned about my whole being. He spent so much time with me, and talked to me and wanted me to be happy. I can still remember the frozen expression on his face whenever I would ask him why I still had the pain. I had my appendix out, and the pain was gone. I had cysts removed from my ovaries, and the pain was gone. Why was the pain not gone after this operation?

I would ask these questions all the time and he would never answer. I would have to learn the answer myself. He knew me so well. He would know how I felt every week by looking at me and feeling my abdomen. He would run blood work constantly and wanted me to be stress free. He did not know about anything going on in my life. He would ask me on several occasions if something had traumatized me in the last two years, but I never answered. I couldn't begin to tell that story. Obviously, my circumstances had contributed to my problems. I was just fortunate to have found this doctor.

I returned once more to the church physician during this time. That was a big mistake. I should have never been examined in the condition I was in. I had been hospitalized for D&C several times while trying to heal from the Crohn's, so it was a vicious cycle to try to recover from both situations. My surgeon was very concerned about my ovaries and kept in contact with my gynecologist often. I did not know how serious things were, and it was foolish of me to return to the church for an examination.

I am saying this to make a point.

I had finished a gynecological examination for the church physician in the city one day and went straight to my doctor on Park Avenue afterward to be checked for the Crohn's surgery. I never said a word to my doctor, as you know. I was so uncomfortable from the church examination that he knew something was wrong with me. He kept asking where I had come from and I broke down and cried. I fell apart and told him the whole story from the beginning and how I had run away and what the church was trying to prove. Et cetera, et cetera.

He was furious! I mean furious. He stood up and pounded his hand on his desk and raised his voice. "Do you honestly think Jesus Christ would want you to be doing this to your body? Do you think Jesus Christ would do this? Become a Methodist, then. You listen to me, young lady, you will never be examined by another doctor from this church as long as you are my patient."

Wow, he was so right. His love for me was so genuine and strained with concern for my life that you could see it all over his face. Nobody had ever fought to protect me like that. He gave me a hug and I wept on his plump shoulders. I loved him like he was my father. I could always sense his love for me. He would always make me call him when I returned home from the city to make sure I got back okay.

This really put him over the top. It was the best thing that could have happened to me. Someone had to put a stop to this insanity with the church physicians, and I hadn't known how to do it. Father Francis had meant so well for me, but enough was enough. My doctor had saved my life once again.

Chapter Nine

I have to admit that opening up to my doctor was an incredible relief. I grew to love and trust him so much, and he genuinely cared about my entire well-being. That is a rare thing to find. I would learn more and more as the years went on that this precious man was truly a gift from God. It made me feel so secure to know someone would take care of me and that I could totally be myself, especially being so sick. He would answer his own phone, and when he saw his patients, there was no clock in the room. He ran the show and was a respected, high-profile surgeon. He was the head of a huge hospital in New York for thirty-five years, so you can imagine that when he spoke, people listened. You can bet even my father respected him.

I continued my weekly visits to the city as I began to recover very slowly. I was becoming more ill with my ovaries and was fighting a major battle in that area.

My father set the court date for my annulment. I had to do everything in my power to stay calm, as this was a major factor for my stomach. My father walked into the courtroom ahead of me, as usual, with his lawyer, and I was alone, as usual. I knew in my heart the only people who cared about me were my mother, my doctor, and Father Francis. I was blessed for that, and I tried to focus on the fact that I was secure in their love for me, even though I sat in that courtroom alone. I was now only nineteen years old, and I would be considered divorced. That was a bad thing back then, and nobody wanted to be labeled with that stigma. The court session began.

Tony sat there with his parents and I sat alone, while my father sat in front of me, telling his lawyer what to do. We had to wait for other cases to be completed, and I had such a knot in my stomach. My heart was so heavy. I didn't know what to expect. When the judge proceeded with our case, all I can remember are a lot of words I couldn't understand and the two attorneys going back and forth, still arguing over who would get a television set. After much deliberation, the judge pounded his hammer on the table, announced who got the television set, and said, "This marriage is now dissolved between the two parties."

It was done. No matter what I had been through, those were the most piercing words I had ever heard. One second, and it was legally over. My father was ecstatic. He turned to his lawyer and said, "What did I tell you? It worked out just like I said." My poor heart sat there alone, crushed, and my father just turned around and said, "Hurry up, let's get out of here." We all left the courtroom, as my father rushed ahead of me with his lawyer, and I remembering walking alone behind them, anxious to get home and cry. Tony looked over to me with a smirk, pleased he got to keep the television and that the war had ended. What a cruel bunch.

It was a painful experience, but nothing compared to the church annulment. That was still in the works. Now I was waiting while reports of their medical examinations were sent to Rome, along with their verbal reports from the chancellery. In the meantime, I continued back to work slowly, beginning with only a few hours a week as I regained my strength. I still experienced abdominal pain, however, not an acute pain as prior to the surgery, but something I would experience for a long time. I waited anxiously, along with Father Francis, for some news from Rome, and finally one day I received my letter.

I must remind you again of my dedication to the Catholic Church. Loving and serving God were the only things I knew. The sacraments were precious to me, and I respected and loved receiving the sacrament of Holy Communion. This was my life. Christ was my life. I was raised to believe that a priest was a representation of Christ, and that is what my heart was anchored in. Again, keep this in mind, as I give you the outcome of my letter from Rome.

I find this difficult to put in words. I honestly cannot describe the pain of what I am about to say. I want you to visualize a young religious girl who truly loved God and wanted forgiveness for running away from her abusive father, not even guilty of the one thing she would be condemned for. I will replay this as vividly as I can recall, which I promise you, it is vivid.

I went upstairs to my bedroom. I opened up the letter from Rome. It was a nightmare to read the conclusion the Church had come to. They discarded me like a piece of old garbage and forbade me from ever receiving the sacraments again. They made it clear that forgiveness from God was not likely and that their decisions were final.

They had continued to read physical reports from doctors regarding my examination, revealing that their findings did not line up with my story. They came to their own conclusions as to whether I was a virgin. They expounded on each physical examination in such an invasive way and discarded every word of truth I had ever spoken to them. They absolutely forbade any kind of annulment, and made sure the lasting impression on my life and soul would be eternal damnation. They got very descriptive of the anatomy of a woman, that only intercourse could have caused this, and that in no way this encounter had not been consummated. I have summed this up as best I can.

I gripped the letter as I read and reread it. Every fiber in my body was shaking. I felt like I was having a bad dream. I literally felt like I was in some sort of hell that was pulling me away from my only hope in life. God Himself. How could this happen? These people and their words represented Christ to me, and what I was feeling was more than a rejection from man, but from God Almighty. In addition to all this anguish, none of this was true. I hadn't consummated this marriage, and even if I had, my God is a God of forgiveness. Why was this happening to me?

I threw myself onto the floor and began to sob uncontrollably. I kept screaming, "No, no, this can't be true, no, no, I need communion, no." You cannot imagine the reality of this letter and the magnitude of being told you can no longer practice being a Catholic, nor receive the sacraments. As I curled up in a ball and continued to cry, my father walked up the stairs. He appeared in his usual anger and asked what was going on. I cried profusely, hardly able to speak, and informed him of what had just happened to me.

He took a quick look at me and said, "That is what you are crying about? The church, the church and God?" On that note, he turned around, and God as my judge, he slapped my face hard to the floor. "Now you have something to cry about." He walked downstairs, leaving me on the floor, sobbing uncontrollably.

I will never forget that day as long as I live. It was as if hell itself had been unleashed upon my mortal body and soul, and there was no hope for recovery. The anguish was beyond words. My sobbing was so bad I couldn't catch my breath—I honestly couldn't breathe. As I was trying to stop crying so I could breathe, something happened that I had never experienced. I heard God Almighty speak to me, and without any control on my part, I stopped crying. He halted my very breath in an instant and a peace overtook my entire being.

He spoke swiftly and clearly: "Susan, DO NOT EVER TRY TO PROVE TO A MAN WHAT I ALREADY KNOW."

That was it. I cannot and will not add to this in any way, shape, or form. This was the voice of God to me. This was truly a visitation from God Almighty. His words would be my comfort and peace, and the weight of condemnation and unforgiveness and hell and damnation had been lifted right off my being. Truly God intervened on my soul and comforted me in the way He saw fit. Nothing physical or earthly could have comforted me and calmed the storm raging in my poor soul that day. It was miraculous, and those words from my precious Lord that day would change my life forever.

CHAPTER TEN

I continued on with my life as best as possible, only now I was closer to God than ever before. I had experienced major awakenings from the Church's rejection, and while some were instant, some would be a process. Father Francis was absolutely beyond devastation. He was heartbroken, and determined to fight what happened to me for the remainder of his calling. He would try to prevent this ever happening to anybody else. I returned to my Italian church within a few weeks after this all happened. I went to Mass and received Holy Communion, and its meaning was even better than before. This was between me and God, and the gates of hell would not prevail. There was a freedom I was experiencing, and a whole new world had opened up for me. I had become convinced that God and the Church were very separate. I couldn't connect the dots of the two being one after all that had happened. My convictions were peaceful, and I grew in my walk with the Lord alone and received the sacrament of Holy Communion just as always. Christ is the head of the Church, not a man.

There were many changes, and one was that I would never go to confession again. I knew I could go straight to God for forgiveness, and no man would be the mediator except Jesus Christ. I was strong in my convictions, and I would continue to operate like someone who was blind but could now see. Yes, it was painful at times—many times—but I thank God, for the strength to go on and the grace to continue. So much fear had been expelled from my life. There was a freedom in God like I had never known before. I knew His love, His forgiveness, and His mercy—everything the Church would not give me. The fear of man and the continual threats from my religion had been like a deliverance from evil itself. I didn't have that fear anymore, just a strong conviction that I would hold on to, and I grew in my faith. I knew God was shedding light on so many different issues. Again, some things would be a process, but believe me when I tell you it was a good one. Truly I was walking with a good God, a tender, sweet, merciful, holy Heavenly Father I had no intention of letting go of. He would protect me. I had something so deep inside of me, and I would nourish that gift for the rest of my life.

I consider myself blessed and fortunate that this evil done against me by the Church was something God turned around for my good. I was concerned for the many hundreds and hundreds, if not thousands, who perhaps turned away from their faith in God because of these men and their doctrines. It was so wrong, and I was powerless to make any of it right. I believe we will all be accountable to God one day, and these rules set up by man, and not God, will not go unpunished. Yes, there are so many excellent priests, and I was fortunate to have known one, but with all his goodness, he was still a small fish in a huge pool of sharks. I am not here to condemn, but to speak of my own experiences in truth. I am here to encourage and strengthen and let people know that their own personal relationship with the Lord is the most important factor. God is so good, and he did not set up these false doctrines and place men in these positions to harm his children. I used to live in fear that if I didn't get to the confessional by Saturday night to confess my sins, hell would be waiting for me Sunday morning if I died. I lived in fear and torment, instead of peace and love.

I know God has established His church, and He built that church on the Rock of Jesus Christ. He wants church to be that sanctuary for the world to come, where His children can feel safe and be set free by truth, not lies. Jesus paid a tremendous price for our freedom and forgiveness, and shame on anyone who sets up their ideas above His. Christ loves the Church, but He will not tolerate the harm it is doing to lives and souls.

I started to read the Bible. We had been taught never to read the Bible as Catholics. I personally experienced the very words of Jesus when He spoke of hypocrites in the book of Matthew, chapter 6: their pride and their places and their posture and the end product of it all. Jesus said, "And when you pray, do not be like the hypocrites, for they love to pray standing in the synagogues and on the street corners to be seen by others" (Matthew 6:5, NIV). When I read these words, I realized I saw and spoke to and watched hundreds of these kinds of men. I had experienced firsthand what Jesus was talking about. God was opening truth to me. Truth is good and not bad. Knowing the truth will set you free. In Matthew 23:23–28 (NIV), Jesus spoke much of the hypocrites. He said:

> Woe to you, teachers of the law and Pharisees, you hypocrites! You give a tenth of your spices—mint, dill and cumin. But you have neglected the

more important matters of the law—justice, mercy and faithfulness! . . . You blind guides. . . . Woe to you, teachers of the law and Pharisees, you hypocrites! You are like whitewashed tombs, which look beautiful on the outside but on the inside are full of dead men's bones and everything unclean. In the same way, on the outside you appear to people as righteous but on the inside you are full of hypocrisy and wickedness.

I knew that wickedness. Again, I just want to speak truth and encourage people, no matter what church or religious organization they are in, to read the scriptures and be enlightened by God's Word as to life and direction. Never be taken by the false traditions of men, who make God's law of no effect. I could go and on, but I have spoken what I know is true, for the sake of truth of the Gospel of Jesus Christ and not man.

CHAPTER ELEVEN

Little by little, the Lord was weaning me out of the Church. It was a process, like I mentioned earlier, but through the grace of God, my walk with the Lord grew closer.

I continued with my weekly visits to New York City to see my surgeon. This particular Friday afternoon in August was a good visit. I always looked forward to seeing him, because he had become a father to me. He knew everything that happened, and he was happy I was getting settled after the agony of church pressure. He was a strong Methodist, which we always joked about because he used to tell me to become a Methodist. I was still in pain, though at least the acute attacks were becoming less frequent.

He was headed out for a month-long vacation. That was scary for me because I was so used to him being around, and this would be the first time he would be gone so long. We said our goodbyes, and I gave him the big hug I always did and told him how much I loved him, and to have a good trip. He informed me to keep in touch with my internist in the village, if necessary. He so looked forward to this vacation every year. He would visit the mountains, which he loved so much. He reminded me to call him as soon as I got home to let him know I was safe.

I arrived home and that was the first thing I did. Nobody had ever looked out for me like this.

He answered his phone as usual: "Are you home safe, young lady?"

I replied, "Yes, Doctor, I'm fine. Have a great trip and hurry back. I love you."

He answered, "I love you too, young lady. And remember, no melted butter and coke syrup if you're nauseous."

He was so awesome. His deep voice from his stocky, plump body always carried authority, and I loved him so.

That was late Friday afternoon. By Monday, I was ill again, and my father had to drive me to the internist. We arrived at the doctor's, and while I was on the examining table he asked me when I had last seen my surgeon. I told him just two days ago before he left for the mountains.

He said, "Susan, he was killed Saturday in a horrific car accident. He and his wife drove off a cliff, and he had a tragic, tragic death."

Oh God no. I jumped off the table and I was in shock. I froze. This doctor grabbed my arm, telling me how it had been a terrible tragedy and that everybody had been devastated with the news. He told me the surgeon loved me like a daughter and how much he always expressed his concern for my well-being.

He said, "I know he was like a father to you and how much you loved and relied on him. I will be here for you now, and I will be a father to you."

Well, naturally, that could and never would be the case. The man for that job was dead. My precious, precious doctor and friend was dead. He wasn't just my doctor, and nobody would ever understand that like I did. He didn't deserve to die like that. That poor man. Oh God, he had saved so many lives, and his was just snuffed away. He radiated love and compassion as a human being, combined with being a major surgeon. Nobody—*nobody*—would ever take his place. A fine family man, now ripped away so tragically.

I sat there, stunned. I couldn't wait to just go home and cry and scream. What would happen to me? Who in the world would I love and love me back and take care of me like this man? He knew my thoughts before I even spoke. He knew my pain before I even told him. Oh God, I was scared. I was so scared. I needed him so much, and he was gone forever. Thank God I had seen him two days ago and hugged him and told him I loved him. My precious special person in my life, never to be replaced.

I still have a letter he wrote to my father about me. It was so beautiful. He told my father I needed a lot of love and that I should always be treated with tenderness and kindness. He expressed to my father his concerns for my future and my health issues and said I would be okay. It went on and on. It was so sincere and so beautiful. It was unimaginable to think how kind he was.

As it turned out, after receiving the bad news, I was rushed directly from the city straight to my hospital near home. My gynecologist was waiting for me because I needed another D&C immediately. I was hemorrhaging and had to be treated. It seemed like I never came up for air, not ever. Between my intestines and my ovaries, I never had one day free of pain. Not one.

Everything was so dark again, and I couldn't even go home to cry. I had to go directly to the hospital. I was so unhappy. All I wanted was my doctor. I was scared and sick, and I wanted him so badly. That poor man, oh God, he didn't deserve this. He had been looking forward to the mountains so much. My heart wanted to die. I felt so sorry this happened to him. What a horrible loss!

I spent three days in the hospital that visit. I was weary and depressed. The battles never ended. I tried so hard to keep up a good attitude, but truthfully, it just never stopped. There weren't times of fun and laughter, and I was tired of doctors and hospitals and being sick. The reports of my future as far as having children were bleak, and it didn't take much to see through the doctors' eyes and their prognosis that I wouldn't have children. I again lived through the eyes of my faith and kept trying not to listen to this constant bad news that circled my life. Father Francis and I were still close friends, and he was always there for me, especially when I was in the hospital. He was still my closest friend, and he would bring me Holy Communion when I was sick. God bless him.

Well, I got out of the hospital and returned to my job in Bronxville. I liked my job, and again, I had a great boss who let me come in whenever I was able. He loved bowling and would come ask me pointers as soon as I got to the office. Remember how I was almost a professional bowler? I enjoyed talking about the game with him, and if there was one thing I knew about, it was bowling. I would have still been bowling had I not gotten ill, and I would have enjoyed some fun at that point, especially competing. I was good at that.

I was almost twenty years old by now, though believe it or not, I felt about fifty. Sickness can definitely change your life. I always had a good sense of humor and was witty and funny, when given the chance. I wasn't around enough people to exercise that humor, except for Father Francis. I would still go the rectory and we would have lunch together and some great talks. I always made him laugh, and he would say, "Suzy Q, don't you ever give up that sense of humor."

It's weird, because he and my gynecologist always called me Suzy. I would even crack jokes about the Church that would make him laugh, and whenever the Italian feast came around, which was a big deal, I would help and hang out with Father.

He wasn't crazy about my new convictions, especially about no more confession, and he would still try to convince me of the things I no longer believed. Aside from that, we had a good, genuine relationship, and we both loved the Lord. We both still respected each other. I had made tremendous progress after the Church rejected me, and each time I walked into church, it became less and less painful. It was hard in the beginning, but I was given the gift to preach from this experience. It was good too! Father would crack up because he knew I was good when it came to talking about the Lord.

If you could possibly believe, in the midst of all this, my adorable mother came home one day and told me how much she loved her hairdresser. We both went to the same hair salon, and I was happy with the guy who did my hair. My mom was beyond the sweetest person in the world. She started telling me I should switch and go to her guy. I was not in the least bit interested. I had the longest, prettiest dark hair. It was the one thing I could be proud of. My doctors always commented on my beautiful, long, dark hair. It was my best feature, and changing a hairdresser was not my concern. I didn't often go to the salon anyway. When I went the next time, my guy wasn't there, so they switched me over to my mother's guy. I couldn't believe it! His name was Joseph. He did my hair and it was fine. No big deal. I went home and my mother was thrilled. Why, I don't know. Anyway, to make a long story short, I went to Joseph to do my hair after that.

One time when I was his last appointment for the day, he asked me to go to the ice-cream parlor next door for an ice cream afterward. Okay, that sounds pretty corny, but truthfully, to me it was great because I was against bars, and getting a date for an ice cream would be rare. What a motivating date. It wasn't over-the-top exciting, but then again, neither was Joseph. I hope you can appreciate my sense of humor when I talk about him, because it just comes with the territory. We went on a few dates after that, and the odd thing is, after I met him, I met another wonderful boy at my job. He asked me out to dinner, about the same time I met Joseph. I hadn't been out in a long time, so this was great. I loved, loved, and still love to dance. Unfortunately, I never met anybody who would fit that tall order for me. I was very conscious of the fact that I had been married, and I thought nobody would think highly of me with that stigma at twenty years old. Nobody would ever even know, unless I told them, but I knew. It bothered me.

My friend, who was named Jordan, was the best date I had ever had. Wow, did he know how to treat me well. He really was a fabulous person. We had a few dates, and I liked him very much. His manners and humor and goodness impressed me. We dated here and there, and he said he wanted to marry me and buy me a beautiful house in Englewood, New Jersey, along with anything I ever wanted for the rest of my life. He meant it too. Just a few dates and I had a decent proposal.

On the flip side of the coin, there was Joseph. I would occasionally go out with him, and I seemed to like him a lot more than Jordan. I liked Jordan, but in a different way. It was more like friendship, and I couldn't see it going any further.

Joe was truly not an exciting guy. I am not being unkind, but it was true. He was quiet and laid back and very opposite from me. Boring, probably, would sum it up. I still don't understand the attraction I felt, and sometimes I think I was just craving the absence of anything close to Tony or my father. I didn't want anybody overpowering or controlling or manipulative, and I think I felt safe in Joseph's corner. Right or wrong, that's where I stayed. My father definitely had a reputation of having money, and since Joseph worked right where I lived, he was well aware of my circumstances (my circumstances being that my father was well off financially). This always left me suspicious that maybe this quiet guy was with me for my father's money. I mentioned earlier how my father was a highly successful—actually, probably the best—real estate broker around and dealt with high-end people, such as the Rockefellers and people from the UN. He also had an exclusive with the movie stars, so he was a smart cookie in his show business and real estate world. He had even purchased a car that had been custom built for Rockefeller.

Anyway, those were my suspicions about Joe. We will call him Joe from here on out. We will leave the name Joseph for the hair salon. He would talk about my father and his reputation for being rich. Everyone had heard about my father. Joe said people in the salon would tell him to date me because my father had money. Who in the world would relay that story to the person they were dating? Joe would. So now my suspicions were confirmed. Nobody would ever believe me because he seemed so quiet and innocent, and that would be his trademark from here on out.

I was in and out of the hospital often, and I came to realize this intestinal problem was here to stay. I got infections frequently and always dealt with anemia between the ovaries and intestine. I eventually had to tell Joe about my medical problems, which I didn't want to do, but I had no choice.

I was now prepared to bring Joe home to meet my father. I was home when the doorbell rang, and when my father answered it, it was Joe. He welcomed him inside and left him in the living room while he walked into the kitchen and said, "What the heck is wrong with his nose? He had a terrible nose job!" Oh well, I guess knowing my father, it could have been worse. Joe would know about his nose soon enough in my family, but apparently, he already knew.

My father was nice to Joe, but he knew without a doubt he could control this guy. Joe was young, but young in a lot of ways, and he looked up to my father because he saw his success and knew he had money. That appealed to Joe. His parents were immigrants and they had had him when they were forty-nine years old.

When Joe was first introduced to my family, my father owned two German shepherds. He had sent the dogs away to be trained to attack whenever my father spoke a special word. Joe was over one evening, and my father had picked up the dogs from their training. He wanted Joe to put on a hat and walk around the back of the house in the dark and pretend he was a burglar. My father would then release the word. Of course, Joe didn't hesitate. Well, off Joe went to be attacked by dogs. Who in the world would have consented to that insanity? Joe. This gives you a brief idea why you need to have a sense of humor when I talk about Joe. My father ate this stuff up. He had found someone who would bow at his every command. Can you imagine an individual like Joe in the hands of my father?

Joe did not have any characteristics of leadership. This was exactly what my father wanted. I personally don't know if I knew what I wanted. I just wanted to be healthy and safe for the rest of my life.

Joe had a sister who had been in a convent for a year. She got out because she wanted to continue smoking. She was a real Catholic, one of those strict ones who never smiled or had any sense of humor. His father, though, was an immigrant and a truly hardworking man who had built a beautiful home and life for his children, considering the language barrier and his ignorance of many things. He worked day and night to provide for his two children. Joe's mother, on the other hand, was a nagging woman who was miserable and bent on spending the rest of her life like that, and she wanted everyone she knew to go down that road. Not the ideal family to marry into, for sure. Marriage was not something that was in the making, but of course, I didn't want to date a lot of guys. Maybe that was a big mistake on my part.

Father Francis was involved as usual. He did not think Joe was right for me in any way. He never stuck his nose where it didn't belong, but I never knew him to be so firm on a conviction like this one. He worried about me, and he didn't want me to be hurt again. He feared I was just seeking the safe zone again, away from my father, and that what I thought was safe was not necessarily safe at all. He was most concerned that I was fighting so much sickness. Time was what I needed, not a man my father could control, because then my father would control both of us instead of just me. Everything was always confusing, and I was afraid to move to the right or to the left. I know I didn't feel secure about myself after what had happened to me, and I also knew sickness constantly hanging over my head made me hate that stigma attached to me also.

I was looking better physically and certainly didn't have any problems getting a date if necessary. Actually, I was looking much better, and quite honestly, a few different people would call me to go out here and there. I was just nervous to get out of the boat. I was a social person, but opportunities didn't arise often, and frankly, I hated the dating scene. I truly wanted to be married and have a family; it was just a matter of finding the right person. I hated the single life. I really did.

I realize I didn't give myself a fair chance, but again, I think Joe was a safety zone from the bad guys, and I chose to stay there. I despised men who ran around like my father, and control freaks and manipulators and cheaters. I favored one quality in Joe: he didn't run around.

CHAPTER TWELVE

I continued to date Joe for two years, and we decided to get married at twenty-one. We would not have any church wedding, of course, and his family, being Italian Catholic, held this against me. Not many people attended, and the ceremony was officiated by a justice of the peace, not anybody we knew. I wore a short dress with a bow in my hair. I will honestly tell you that this ceremony was worse than a funeral. The only attendants were the justice of the peace (a stranger); Joe's mother, father, and sister, who looked like they just got off the boat from Italy; my mother and father; and two witnesses. It was very cold, and the person I wanted there most, Father Francis, did not attend. I was so disappointed, but Father would not come. To this day, I don't know why. We never stopped our friendship for a moment, but he would not attend this ceremony. He was not in favor of the wedding at all.

Frankly, I was scared to marry again. I still believe I could have used more time to heal, but there were many factors involved, the main one, of course, being that the possibility of having children was slim if I waited. We were both young, to say the least, but we married anyway. We lived in his parents' three-family house on the third floor for five years, and not to get into details, it was a difficult situation for me. New couples should not live in the same house with their family, no matter who it is. I was very sick at times, which was nothing new, but I continued to work between being hospitalized continually.

I finally did get pregnant, and after two years, I had my little boy, Thomas Joseph. It was a difficult pregnancy, but my precious little boy arrived. Father Francis baptized him in the Italian Catholic church. I did not want to raise him Catholic, but I didn't know any alternative at that time and just continued with my faith in God and not man. Thomas, or Tommy, would be my pride and joy for the rest of my life. He was the sweetest little baby boy anyone could have prayed for, and he was an absolute answer to prayer. My mom and Father Francis were my best friends, and I lived in this old Italian community, so it wasn't likely I would meet any friends my age in this neighborhood. I would take Tommy to my mother's house, where we would adore him. She had a great yard, so he would have a good time playing.

The living situation with my in-laws was becoming more stressful and we were looking for a house upstate, where we would begin our lives in our own lovely home. My dad, being the real estate broker he was, found us a beautiful home up the line about forty-five minutes from our parents, which was in a private lake area. I was thrilled to be moving away from my in-laws, and the only one I would miss being close to was my mother. It really was a lovely, lovely home, and we would spend the next twenty-five years there raising our children. I could not have asked for a better home. Tommy enjoyed the acre of property, and we cherished the beautiful lake across the street. I still had to travel to my doctors down county, but I managed quite well. Father Francis would visit often, but soon after that he was transferred to New York City. Our lives would soon go in different directions, but we always stayed in touch. He was transferred to a prominent position as the head over hundreds of priests. He now would have a huge influence in the church and their decisions regarding situations, such as mine regarding annulments. How ironic was that? I certainly wish he had been in that position before, but God was in control. Father Francis was right where he was for me all those years.

Chapter Thirteen

I was now twenty-three years of age, married two years and the mother of a little boy. We were enjoying our home very much, and Tommy was finding his new playmates in a young fresh community. I loved the house, and I myself was finding friends my age. We enjoyed our children playing and growing up together. I certainly hate to be repetitious about my illnesses, but unfortunately, I cannot leave that out. I was anxious to have another child, along with fighting my doctors' mutual consensus otherwise. I suffered with my ovarian problems, along with my intestine disorders, and when I became very ill at times, my mother was always there to help. I was confident and diligent in my faith, and I was determined to have another child. That conviction was anchored in my soul, and my doctors were very much agitated by my hesitation to have my ovaries removed. I did eventually get pregnant, and I had a gorgeous girl named Juliane. I could not have asked for more perfect children, especially having a boy and a girl. I had desired to have a boy first because I wanted him to protect his sister, and to this day, those dreams have come true. He could not have been a better brother to Julie since she was born. She was a tough cookie from day one. She was born with an independent spirit and was cleaning her room before she was two. She was so pretty, but she was a strong-willed girl from birth. We had a beautiful baptism for Julie in the house, and Father Francis came up from the city to baptize her. It was lovely. There was an age difference of four years between Tommy and Julie. They were my pride and joy and my miracle babies.

When Julie turned eight months old and Tommy was close to turning four, I had to have a total hysterectomy. I mean total! I was quite ill, and without my mother, I never could have survived. I could not pick up the baby for three months, so my mom lived with us and took care of the children and me. When a doctor gives you a total hysterectomy at twenty-six without any preparation for the outcome, trust me—it's definitely total. Not only are your ovaries and uterus removed, but included is your entire well-being, your mind, body, and soul. It was a hell I wouldn't wish on anybody. I never was informed of the consequences of surgical menopause and what would be involved for my future.

It was quite evident the entire operation had been necessary because of the confirmation of past surgeries and several doctors. They said they had tried to save even a part of my ovary, but that had not been possible. I do believe it, because at that point I could no longer walk or endure the high fevers, pain, and blood loss.

I walked into that hospital one person, and after that surgery, I walked out another. I was already battling Crohn's disease on a daily basis, which had caused several neurological problems to surface. Now I left that hospital going through an instant life change, with two little children at home. My doctors never told me what to expect. The doctor walked into the hospital room every day after the surgery and asked me if I felt different yet. I had no idea what he was talking about. I was oblivious to the surgery's outcome; I was just looking forward to the physical pain being gone. The pain from my ovaries was gone forever, but the emotional roller coaster that was about to begin and the physical changes that had already started were absolutely frightening. I am definitely a person who has experienced physical and mental pain. Both are horrible.

The changes in my body began to spiral out of control, and the depression, the crying and unhappiness, terrified me. I had been a happy person, and now I was catapulted into a darkness I never knew possible. Four days had passed since the surgery, and by the fifth day I didn't know what had hit me. Nobody had explained what I was to expect after waking up to menopause. I was sweating and shaking and crying, and the depression was consuming me. This was so out of character for me because I was such a positive person. I had absolutely no control of what was happening to me. My gastroenterologist, who was a wonderful, brilliant doctor, told me what I was feeling was like a man having his testicles cut off. He was direct when he spoke, and he didn't mince words. He also sat in on the surgery, because of my Crohn's, and he was very kind to me and concerned that my stomach would flare up because of these symptoms.

They began estrogen therapy several times a day, and I was so concerned about my children and what condition I would be in when I left the hospital. I was so anxious to get home to them, yet I feared what was happening to me. When I returned home, it took three months before I was able to pick up my daughter. It was a long recovery, and the road ahead would be another long and dark one, only this time, I had two precious children to raise.

I can't describe the reality of waking up one day and having your entire world turned upside down. My life was an emotional roller coaster. I still can't believe to this day that my gynecologist had never prepared me for this kind of mental anguish.

CHAPTER FOURTEEN

The next year was, without a doubt, one of the most difficult years of my life. I emphasize the result of this surgery for the sake of many women out there who have also experienced surgical menopause at a young age. Depression is an absolutely horrible place to be. It doesn't matter why or how you got there, but I sympathize so deeply with those who suffer this darkness. I have, as I mentioned earlier, experienced physical and emotional pain, and both are terrible, but there is a dimension of suffering in the emotional realm that, unless you have been there, you cannot even understand. I felt like my happiness had been snatched away forever, and the crying spells that would come on without any control were crippling. I did not know what to expect moment to moment. My mother was everything to me through this, and my children were the reason I could even get up in the morning. I do not believe I would have survived this horror without my faith in the Lord Jesus Christ. Having faith does not make a situation easier, but it will make the impossible possible. I leaned heavily upon the Lord. Joe, however, was not very patient as a young husband. This situation wasn't easy for any man, but I am a firm believer that love will get you through anything and everything. Joe could be the most patient man in certain situations, but sickness and responsibility were things he wanted nothing to do with. The burden, then, was on my mother.

As if the hormonal problems weren't already enough, I developed neurological problems through all this. Between this and Crohn's disease, my health was always in poor condition. Please let me say this: anybody who ever knew me would never know of my health issues, unless they were close friends. To this day, by the grace of God, I am particular about my looks and my figure, and I am a real fashion freak. Even on my worst days, Joe never came home from work and found me in pajamas. My personal appearance, my home, and my children were also kept beautifully. The friends I did have could not believe that I would polish my furniture looking like Donna Reed. I was dressed with earrings on and always looked like I was stepping out somewhere. I am proud to be like that, and I still am. It doesn't matter whether it's important to a spouse; it's important to me.

I was under the care of several physicians, including a neurologist and neurosurgeon, and I had five myelograms in four years because of the terrible pain occurring throughout my body. I also spent time at the Cleveland Clinic trying to be diagnosed for this severe problem. I had nerve blocks in my head, acupuncture, and was tested for lupus and several other issues. My life was horrible, to say the least, and to be quite honest, Julie and Tommy were the only reasons I wanted to live. No, I didn't want to die—if anything I had a continual fight to live—but what I am saying is that my children were the reason I fought so hard to live. I wanted to be well for them. My marriage was not good, and that had little to do with my being sick.

Father Francis visited me often in the hospitals and tried to counsel with Joe and myself on marital issues. It really was not good. Joe worked hard and we had a beautiful home, but he did not want the responsibility of a family. He had said it quite often, but in spite of it, he was a good father when the children were young. I was the disciplinarian in the family, and I always would be, especially when they became teenagers. I will not be specific in the details of our unhappy marriage out of respect for my children, who love their father. I would not want it any other way.

CHAPTER FIFTEEN

I continued with estrogen therapy while Joe went to work, and we raised our children. I had to have breast surgery in the interim because of all the estrogen, and by the time I was in my early thirties, several doctors wanted me to discontinue it, including the breast surgeon. My doctors in the city also agreed, and if you can believe this, I was removed from estrogen therapy in my early thirties, with no other alternative. I got off it cold turkey and withdrew from it like a heroin addict. I went through all the symptoms that came with detoxing, and I did it all alone in my house raising my children. It was horrific! I remember holding on to the backboard of my bed from the shaking. I still cannot believe I survived that first year.

Over the years to come, I would be stricken with severe osteoporosis from the lack of estrogen. My neurological problems were diagnosed as fibromyalgia, which became debilitating at times. My intestinal disorders were brutal, and my quality of life was not good.

I mention again that nobody would know this by looking at me, and I am so thankful to God for His grace. I never wanted to be connected to sickness, and nobody ever knew what my real life was like. I could never travel or vacation because of my stomach, but my life was my family and I was thankful for that. The children were very involved in school activities, and I was so happy they could have a social life growing up in a public school, the life I never had. They had twirling, soccer, cheerleading, football, music, and fun. They were both so talented, and everything they did made me so proud. They worked at a young age making their own money, and they really were exceptional and responsible. Julie babysat at a young age, and my son cut lawns and shoveled snow. He eventually bought his own tractor and had his own little job in the neighborhood that would allow him to save up for a car. They were great kids, and I looked forward to each activity so much.

Tommy and Julie are the greatest blessings in my life, then and now and forever. Their cheerleading and football games and ice skating at the lake, all the wonderful activities they were involved in, were the best moments of my life. The teenage years, however, were not my favorite, because of all the outside influence and driving and little by little knowing less and less about their whereabouts.

I was thankful my faith in God had given me a positive attitude. I fixed my eyes on the good things and was always optimistic. Joe, however, was the opposite. I am not putting him down, but stating a major factor that can ruin a relationship. He had so much to be thankful for, but he thrived on anything negative. Before I had my children, he was annoyed with me for wanting and trying so hard to conceive Julie and Tommy when the doctors had already pronounced doom. I would not go down the negative road. However, that is easier said than done. We never saw anything the same, and most of the time, that was the root of the problem. Another factor was that I was affectionate and Joe was not. He was in his own world, and I really did raise my children as a single parent, with Joe being physically there but not involved.

We quarreled often, and it could get bad. I would not allow the word "divorce" to be said in our house, and it was not an option or a thought, at least on my part. Father Francis was trying to help us, but we were two people who just could not get along. I mention once again that nobody — *nobody* — knew my personal business on the outside. Everybody thought Joe was a great guy and we were a happy couple. I did not speak to girlfriends or my mother or outsiders, other than Father Francis, about my situation. I hated gossip, and people just judge you anyway.

I had hit the bottom, and things just became worse. I had been released from Columbia Presbyterian Hospital in the city after being very ill, and for the first time in my life I honestly didn't know if I was going to live long. I was sick and weak and frail, but never before this had I thought I would die. I was scared and ill, and my mom came up to stay with me as usual. I had been in the bedroom and overheard Joe and my mother speaking in the living room. Joe was telling my mother he wanted no part in taking care of me, and my poor, tired mother said she needed to go home and be with my father. I was a complete mess, and honestly, at that point, hearing that conversation, I wanted to die if it had not been for Julie and Tommy. I was petrified that if I did die, my children would be raised by my father. This is the gospel truth. There was no fight left in me except the will to save my children from being raised by that man. I threw myself at the hands of God and cried out for Him to heal me so I could see my children grow up. I begged God to not let me die, because of Julie and Tommy. I knew the Lord had given them to me, and I knew he wanted me to be well and raise them. I was just so weak and tired, and the love I had never received from my father, and Tony, would now be shifted to rejection by Joe. My marriage was horrible, and my world was falling apart once again. I turned to the one and only true help as usual—my Lord and Savior Jesus Christ!

It was a Thursday morning in October. I wept hard in my bedroom, recalling the conversation the night before between Joe and my mother. My mother was so precious and had meant no harm, but she was always the one who had to pick up the pieces when it came to taking care of somebody. She never thought of herself, but she was tired also and just wanted to go home.

Joe, on the other hand, was my husband. He had shifted me and all this responsibility onto my mother from the beginning. I was sick of being a burden, when quite frankly, the only burden was a negative husband who wanted no part in raising his family. That was a huge burden on me, and there was nothing I could do about it.

I cried out to God, and the phone rang. It was a friend in the neighborhood, and she asked me to go with her to a prayer meeting at the Catholic church that night. She said she would pick me up, as she knew I was ill. I hesitated, especially about going back to the Catholic church, but I had not been in church for years and I didn't know anything else. I wanted to go, so we went.

The church was a contemporary church around the lake. It was a powerful evening, and I was so happy to be there. The prayer meeting was so powerful, and I no doubt met the Lord in a deeper way that evening. I was touched by God in my spirit, and encouraged and strengthened in a supernatural way. God had ordained that night and visited me. It was a changing point in my life forever. People prayed for me, and that night would be a new beginning. I knew I would live and not die. God opened doors for me to sing and play my guitar again, and I was leading the music in the healing masses and prayer meetings and Bible studies.

God had truly revived my spirit. I was so miraculously healed in my soul, and I threw myself in the Word of God like never before. I read and read the Bible and prayed for hours for myself and others. I prayed for Joe and my marriage, and I had such direction in my life. My physical problems were the same, but I grew in a deeper faith from reading the Bible. I knew if I believed and had faith in God, He would make me well. I had direction for Julie and Tommy, and I deposited God's Word into them now at a young age, giving them Christ and all His love. Joe was not interested in any of God's plan, even though I wanted so much for him to get on board because I knew God wanted to heal our marriage. Still, he was not interested. It was so sad. Father Francis tried talking to Joe again, but Joe wanted no part of God or helping our lives. At that point, Father Francis got annoyed with him. He was stern and told Joe he was sick of the fact that I was continually reaching out every day for the grace of God, while Joe was constantly refusing it. He said I needed to be loved and that Joe's rejection of God and me was going to be a disaster if he didn't try to love me and hold me and show some sort of affection.

Joe and I didn't have a life together as far as any type of physical connection. We had conceived our two children, but that was the extent of it. I know that is personal, but I guess I didn't come this far not to tell it all. I didn't want to, but this is the truth. Joe was disinterested in being a husband in every sense of the word. The marriage was a mistake from the beginning, and now I would be the one on a mission to save it, with God's help. You can imagine the loneliness and rejection I was living with on a continual basis.

There were no other women. Joe wasn't interested in me, or other women, or his children, or anything. He is exactly that way today, and there is nothing anybody can do about it. The pressure was on me all the way. Well, getting back to what I said in the beginning: He definitely wasn't like my father, which was a good thing, but he wasn't my safety zone, either.

CHAPTER SIXTEEN

I was so thankful for my appreciation for music. Singing and writing songs were a very important part of my life. Focusing on music was always a great passion of mine, and would lead me to making my own CD.

I had left the Catholic church after a couple years, and raised Julie and Tommy in the nondenominational church. It was different from the Catholic church, but quite frankly, still legalistic. It was a good Bible-based church, and teaching my children the Bible was first and foremost. The church activities were good for them. Joe was removed from all of it, but that would not stop me from being the spiritual leader of the home. I would take the children to church and all that was involved, and continue to act like a single mother when decisions had to be made. The teenage years, of course, were not my favorite. My children were good kids, but that is not the point. You have to be on your toes with teenagers. I give credit to God for their safety through those years of pressure from all the outside world. They knew Joe and I never agreed on anything and that our marriage was not good. Joe would disappear to his mother's house more frequently because the strife was becoming unbearable. Father Francis tried to help, but Joe did not want any part of it.

Tommy finally graduated high school and Julie was in her prime teenage years at fifteen years old. Tommy attended a local community college for two years and commuted back and forth while working various jobs at the same time. The pressure was definitely building in our home, and one day when I came home from the driving range with my son, Joe had left for good. I will never forget that day. It was the spring of 1990, and everything he had always wanted from the beginning, he had done. He did not want to be married and have responsibility, so now with Tommy as a young man, he had decided to leave. As much as our lives were not good, I never wanted to go on in life with anybody else. I was absolutely petrified because I had never been alone or worked or supported myself, and I knew no other life except Joe, even if we were not happy together. As much as I fought all my illnesses, I was no doubt the strength and leader of this family, even if I didn't make the money. However, I still had so many weaknesses, and that was the root of my dependence on Joe. It was strange because he didn't take care of me when I was ill, but I guess I never knew anything else but this life we had built, good or bad.

The stress was making my issues worse, and now I was left in this big home with my children. Our marriage had failed all the way. I will always remember when he told me over and over that he didn't love me and hadn't ever loved me. He said he did not want to be married and that he did not want the responsibility of any of us anymore. I begged him—and I mean begged on my knees—for him not to divorce me and send me out into this crazy world at forty-six years old as a single woman. I didn't date young, and I certainly wasn't going to now. We had been married twenty-five years, and now it was over.

Well, over was not quite the way it went. It was the beginning of another ugly war, where lawyers are involved and get rich. I refused to sign divorce papers and break this covenant with God or Joe, but I had no choice in the matter. It got bad. Joe, who had appeared to be a nice, quiet guy and a good man, now turned on me and did to me what I never could possibly have expected. When you don't want to be married anymore, that is bad enough, but dragging and demoralizing a person you were with for twenty-five years is a whole other issue. I was ripped apart by his attorney. He was going to make this a hell for me that I did not deserve. He would not blink at never seeing Julie and Tommy, and as usual placed all demands on his son, who, by the way, to this day takes responsibility for his family.

Tommy had graduated community college by now and was going to start at SUNY Albany for his last two years. My health was seriously affected by the separation, and nobody was there for me but my son, my daughter, and my one best girlfriend. Churches and Christians were, without a doubt, not there for me in this time of need, especially divorce. It doesn't matter what denomination, people—supposedly God's people—are the most judgmental. I will not make excuses for them, but I will speak boldly that I was so mistreated during this divorce. I was alienated because they said divorced people were going to hell. It was no different from the Catholics, just another group of hypocrites who sang their songs and claimed to sing His praises, but there is no love in them. What a journey I was on now. Thank God I had established my own walk with the Lord and never counted on pastors and people in the Church.

I was taking this whole matter badly, and my father, as you could well imagine, was the worst of my enemies. I would call him crying from the devastation, and God is my judge, this is what my father said to me: "Don't call me again. I like Joe, and I will come up to that house and hit you over the head with a baseball bat." He was the same horrible father he always was. I was alone, scared, and sick and at the mercy of Joe giving me money. From then on, my son would bear the brunt of being the man of the house.

CHAPTER SEVENTEEN

Well, I will say this proudly: though the situation was terrible, God had given me a son who would step into this role and never turn back from taking care of his mother. There are not enough books I could ever write to praise this young boy who turned into the greatest man I would ever know and respect.

I will make this as brief as possible, and try not to drag out all the details. My son, who was supposed to start his third year of college at SUNY Albany, stayed out for two years while this hell went on. He worked and took care of me and Julie, and took on the role of a husband at nineteen years old. He also was a father to Julie, who at the time was fifteen years old and a teenager in the middle of her parents' divorce. Tom had a full-time job working and taking care of the house, me, and Julie. He was the most amazing young man you could ever imagine. He was devastated that he had postponed college, but he met his present obligations and confronted them head on. My doctors were so impressed with his responsibility, and they would tell me candidly that he would turn out better than their kids, who got everything handed to them. I will tell you honestly that I would never have made it without my son.

I stayed alone in my lovely home with my children for four years. It was sad, and Joe didn't see the children except to meet my son and give him the money. There was so much strife now with the lawyers involved, and now what had been a twenty-five-year relationship resolved itself to be nothing more than a financial agreement between two people. It was disgusting. Joe was willing to work to give all this money to lawyers, and that is exactly what happened. My father could not have been worse, and only my children were my salvation, as usual. It was a sad time, and it was hard to believe it was happening to me and not somebody else. Especially divorce. Living through a divorce after twenty-five years, I can honestly understand why God said He hates divorce. It is a painful experience, especially for the one who did not initiate it or want it.

Three years had passed since Joe left us, and now in the fall of 1993, I put the house up for sale. My life there had been spent with much sorrow, and getting out of that house was Lazarus coming out of the grave. My beautiful home sold quickly, and in six weeks I had to be out. I sold everything, and I mean everything. I needed money, and everything was gone in six weeks. I remember selling a beautiful twelve-piece set of china for two hundred dollars. Our beautiful pool table, all our furnishings, everything was gone. The divorce was not final yet, but the lawyers were making out very well.

CHAPTER EIGHTEEN

Everything had to be out of the house by February 1994, and the closing was set for that same time. Keep in mind, I am not expounding on the horrible details and terror involved in having to be out of your house by a certain date with no place or plan in sight. I will expound, however, to the fact that I was walking by faith and that this was probably one of the toughest tests of my walk with God. I was trusting Him, but also experiencing the frightening fact that there was absolutely no door opening for me. My daughter was in college in Albany, and my son was waiting to return to college too. My children were in a panic, and rightfully so. I recall my daughter saying we were all going to be out on the street because the house was sold, and I was pushing my faith too far. My attorney told me I was going to be a bag lady. (I would like to mention that I was certainly a bag lady in the fact that I opened two designer-handbag boutiques down the line.) I didn't have a positive force around me except my faith and the best friend in the world to this day whom I had met at church. She permeated Christ in her entire life and was a prayer warrior for my life and my family. She pulled me through the hardest circumstances, and to this day still does. I didn't have a lot of friends, but I would not have traded the quality in this one woman for anybody in the world.

We went through the holidays, and February was upon us. I had cleared out everything and still had no idea where I was going. The pressure was on, and I kept pressing into God for direction, but still nothing. I will plainly tell you I had never been so scared in my life, mainly and solely for the purpose that I was petrified that my children would go off somewhere and I would have to live with my father. That was always my biggest nightmare. It appeared this was the only possible way out, but I was praying and begging that God would forbid that cup to ever enter my life again. My father was truly a horrible and mean man, and I had come to realize he and Joe had become my mortal enemies and nobody would ever understand this like I would. They had both betrayed and left me, and the last four years had been a hell I would never have endured if I had a good father and husband. Divorce was bad enough, but once again, my father was never there for me. The position he took with Joe was just another indication that my life would be better off far away from them both. Truly my enemies were in my household.

Obviously, God Almighty felt the same way. I was nearing the end of the month, and the closing on the house was about to take place. I picked up the local pennysaver in our area, which included many ads. Little did I know my destiny was waiting for me in that little newspaper. I was not searching for anything in particular, but an advertisement for a beautiful, fully furnished condo on the beach caught my attention. Immediate occupancy was available, and no pets were allowed. The condo was in Myrtle Beach. I had never been there before, but my daughter's boyfriend had been attending the Citadel in Charleston, South Carolina, so she had heard of the area before. I grasped the ad and felt comfortable in following this lead. One month. I didn't have many details, but I had a strong conviction as the days went on that this was where God was leading me. I had always wanted to move to the South, but this was something that seemed like a temporary fix for as soon as the house sold. I would have a limited amount of funds, and I had to move quickly. I also had two little Yorkies. They were my other children. Where would they go and what would I do with them?

I moved out in faith on this ad, and things started to come together. Each step was a God-given miracle. It was amazing to see how He ordained and orchestrated this departure for me. I would leave with my daughter three days after we got out of our house, and I would stay with my parents for only three days. Julie and I would leave on a flight and she would take off a semester from college and go with me. She was thrilled because her boyfriend was living there. Tommy would finally go forward and finish up his last semester in Albany.

What a nightmare, but it was finally coming to an end. The battle was huge, but I can boldly proclaim my God brought an incredible victory for me and my children at the last minute. I will be forever grateful, and I will never forget it. I could never have pulled this off in a million years. My friends took my Yorkies, and all I could do was take one day at a time, as usual. I knew I had only one month, but I needed such restoration at that point that only God knew the rest I needed. The closing was finalized. I got my portion of settlement, which was very little in piecemeal, and I walked away from my house with nothing but a suitcase. Tommy left for Albany, and Julie and I stayed at my parents for three days.

The three days there with my father were horrific. I was at the end of my rope. I had had enough of New York and Joe and my father and my entire life there, and I had never wanted to get on a plane so badly in my life and leave and never come back.

We arrived at the airport, and when that plane took off, I felt like God had delivered me from a lifelong hell. I never wanted to see New York or my father or Joe ever again. I was like Abraham. I didn't know what was ahead for me, and I had left everything I had ever known. Leaving my mother was the hardest thing in the world for me. I had no idea when or if I would ever return, but as the story goes, I left with one suitcase and sold everything I had. I lost my home and my family and my mother and father. To get right to the point, I never returned to New York, except to finalize my divorce and to see my parents for the last time. God had taken me away from all of them and given me a new beginning. I missed my best friend and mother, and that would be the extent of all I cared about in New York.

My girlfriend and her husband drove down to South Carolina a month later with my little Yorkies. Each month, God opened up a new place for me to stay. I never had anything mapped out or planned except walking out an incredible journey of faith with an incredible God who never failed me or forsook me. The door was forever shut in New York, but He had opened up a Red Sea for me that I would never forget. Nobody can deny how His mighty Hand and wondrous works led me out of that wilderness forever! Truly, my Maker is my Husband (Isaiah 54:5).

CHAPTER NINETEEN

After departing from New York in a terrible ice storm, it was a beautiful contrast arriving in balmy South Carolina. It was the beginning of March, and the South was more desirable than all my years experiencing those cold winters. My rented condo overlooked the ocean, and it was beyond what I could have expected. The view was spectacular, and it certainly would be my haven for the next month as I continued to walk by faith. Tommy would arrive that following May, after graduating college in Albany, and Julie would finish her college years in the South working on her career in music.

While Tommy prepared for law school, I was finally able to complete my contemporary Christian CD, all written and performed by me. I was excited to sing in the local churches and for Christian TV whenever the opportunity arose.

The South became a permanent home for all of us, and I couldn't have been more grateful.

CHAPTER TWENTY

Several years passed, and Tommy finished law school and was settled in Atlanta. I was still living in South Carolina, where I ran a handbag boutique. I kept in touch with my parents as much as possible, especially since my mother had dementia. It was hard to communicate with her, so of course, each phone call had to be channeled through my father. It was difficult for me to travel alone for health reasons, so I was unable to return to New York.

This one particular time, Tommy flew from Atlanta to pick me up, and we both flew to New York to see my parents. My girlfriend picked us up at the airport and we went up to my parents' apartment. It was sad to see what had transpired over the years. My father, who had been a brilliant business man, had lost all their belongings, including their beautiful home, because of his gambling addiction. He looked old and haggard, and my mother was sitting in a corner talking to herself on the couch. They hardly had any furniture, and on the stove there was pot with canned sauce that looked three days old. My mother was so neglected. There were other family members who would always be there for them, but unfortunately, their lives had spiraled out of control by this point. There was nothing anybody could do.

I have to admit, I was excited to see them both, but to my disappointment, again, my father paid little attention to me and instead focused in on my girlfriend. I guess old habits are hard to break. When you are a womanizer young, you will be a womanizer old. He took the only thing left of their belongings—an old beaver coat of my mother's—and gave it to my girlfriend.

We took them to dinner and tried to spend as much time with them as possible in the few days we were there. My other friend cooked them a lovely dinner, but nothing would make my father enjoy our time together. He was miserable and rude and ungrateful. He was putting me down as usual, and he was bossy and demanding to Tommy, who by this time was doing all he could to control himself.

It was Sunday morning, our last day in New York before our flight home on Monday. We would fly to South Carolina, and from there Tommy would continue back to Atlanta. I wanted to spend every minute of that last day with my mother, but my father told us to go home. I explained that we only had one more day there, but he didn't care how he treated us.

To make a long story short, he told us to get out and that we hadn't been welcome in the first place. I resorted to begging my own father to let me see my mother, but he continued to refuse. As we got ready to leave, I went over to hold my mother for the last time and tell her how much I loved her. Tommy finally broke through my father's continual verbal abuse. He said, "You will never, never see your daughter again." We walked out of the apartment, my father slamming the door behind us.

I broke down and wept in the gloomy hallway. This was going to be the last time I saw my parents. I had that whole day to spend time with them, but instead Tommy and I drove around in the pouring rain and flew home the following day. It had not been easy for Tommy to leave his new position as an attorney, and it hadn't been easy for me with my health situation.

Both my parents went into a nursing home after that. My father died before my mother, so of course, with her condition, she never knew he passed. I spoke to my father every night at seven o'clock in the nursing home, right up until he died. I never hung up without telling him I loved him, even though he never, ever told me back.

It never had to end like this for either one of them, especially my beautiful mother.

I would never return to New York again. Shortly after, I myself moved to Atlanta, and my daughter did also. I opened a beautiful designer-handbag boutique in the area and was thrilled at being able to operate in the things I loved: buying merchandise and preparing for the opening of my new store. Things had started to look up, and now I would focus on my future home in Atlanta, where I was so happy to be living. The energy was great, and the excitement of a new beginning with new friends, along with my children, was another victory to be celebrated.

Afterword

Alpharetta, Georgia, is to me the perfect place to live. It is a beautiful suburb of Atlanta and has everything to offer in regard to stores and location and activities. I enjoyed my boutique for a few years, and I continue today to write and compose songs. My children are settled into their careers, and thankfully, we all live in the same area. We presently have a second home in South Carolina at the beach, which gives us access to the best of both worlds as a family. We have truly been blessed with a double portion, and beyond all that, knowing that God holds tomorrow and He holds my hand.

About the Author

Susan Sansalone now resides in Alpharetta, Georgia. Her children also reside there and have settled into their careers. Her son is a prominent attorney, and her daughter an accomplished musician and piano teacher. Susan is still involved in writing her own songs and continues her passion for music and fashion. While she's remained single, she has always kept her desire for a godly husband. She continually thanks God for holding her feet and her children's feet to His path.